Enlightenment in Our Time

Second Edition

Winter 2012

Lonny J. Brown, HHC

for Olya
Happy New Year!
LJB

First Edition published 2001 - ISBN 1-931391-86-6

Manufactured in the United States of America.

Enlightenment Projects
2007

ENLIGHTENMENT PROJECTS
Peterborough, NH, 03458 USA
www.LonnyBrown.com
lonny@holistic.com

Enlightenment in Our Time

The Perennial Wisdom
in the
New Millennium

Lonny J. Brown, HHC

Thank You:

Paramahansa Yogananda, Chogyam Trungpa Rinpoche,
Ram Dass, H.H. The Dalai Lama,
and all the Enlightenment Ones,
who cared enough to teach.

With Great Love to Danny-Sue Almitra

Enlightenment is real..
not fantastic,
not for an elite, but for all of
humanity.

Sogyal Rinpoche

TABLE OF CONTENTS

FOREWORD 1
DEDICATED TO LOVE 3
LIFE'S COSMIC LITTLE SECRETS 5
WHAT IS THIS UNIVERSE? 7
BUT FIRST, A QUICK REALITY CHECK 11
ULTIMATE QUESTIONS 13
THE MANY NAMES OF ENLIGHTENMENT 16
ENLIGHTENMENT IN OUR TIME 21
SCIENTIFIC MYSTICISM 26
BARKING UP THE RIGHT TREE 30
TO HEAL THE SOUL 35
THE ABSOLUTE POWER OF MIND 40
SYMPTOMS OF ENLIGHTENMENT 42
CRAZY WISDOM STRIKES AGAIN 48
THE FOREST & THE TREES: TRANSCENDING DUALITY 49
BEGIN WHERE YOU ARE 57
WAYS OF TRANSFORMATION 58
THE YOGA OF LIFE 59
MEDITATION: THE SEAT OF ENLIGHTENMENT 61
ENLIGHTENMENT IN YOUR BODY 69
TEACHERS ARE MIRRORS 85
VISUALIZATION: SEEING YOUR WAY THROUGH 99
YOUR PSYCHIC ENERGY CENTERS 102
DREAMS ARE RELATIVELY REAL 116
SACRED SUBSTANCES: THE FLESH OF THE GODS 118
WHAT'S LOVE GOT TO DO WITH IT? 120
ENLIGHTENMENT ONLINE 122
SPIRITUAL PEST CONTROL 131
ENLIGHTENMENT AND EVIL 136
PERILS ON THE PATH 138
SURVIVE & THRIVE / HEAL & BE HEALED 141
SACRED SEX 147
WHY DEATH IS NOT A PROBLEM 154
REAL COMMENTS FROM REAL FRIENDS 172
APPENDIX 183
BIBLIOGRAPHY 192
ABOUT THE AUTHOR 197

FOREWORD

If you've ever wondered what life is all about, Lonny Brown has the answer: enlightenment. That's not a new answer, of course; it is actually millennia old. Although it has many names - liberation, God-realization, non-dual consciousness, moksha, satori - it is the unanimous declaration of the world's major religions and sacred traditions. Enlightenment, they agree, is what life --both for the individual and for the human race - is all about. Enlightenment is discovering our ultimate unity with the source of existence and living in accordance with it. It is the way to enduring happiness and true understanding of reality. But each age must rediscover it for itself so that it remains relevant and not the dead words of past authority.

Now, many others have written about enlightenment in the present age, including me. Often, however, the presentation is highly abstract, lofty and difficult to comprehend intellectually. Lonny has written a simple book of living wisdom. In the short chapters awaiting you, he presents enlightenment in many of its aspects and applications, and he does so in a practical way.

Theory is fine; many people write about enlightenment in theory. Without practice, however, theory remains unapplied and unable to deliver the benefits as you grow in spiritual understanding toward an enlightened state of mind. If enlightenment is a kingly banquet, Lonny doesn't want you to stand outside looking at it through a window; he wants you to come inside and taste the glorious feast. So he offers advice - short, simple, practices and ideas - to make the theory real for you personally. He invites you to partake and be spiritually nourished.

There is more to enlightenment than Lonny covers here. He'll be the first to acknowledge that. Enlightenment is a subject as vast as the universe and as close as your breath; you can't cover all that in a short book such as this. Then again, you couldn't cover all that in a long book either - or even in a thousand long books. So this is a wonderful place to start, to take a first step on your journey of a thousand miles. As you progress, you'll discover that a loving cosmos will provide all you need, every step of the way. The important thing is to actually take that first step.

With Lonny as your guide, you can "make haste slowly," at a self-paced rate. That way, your practice will deepen your understanding of the theory, which in turn will feed back to solidify your practice. The distinction between theory and practice will dissolve as the quest for enlightenment - for living as your authentic self - encompasses all aspects of your existence. You'll find that you undergo changes on all levels of your being. Those changes will be for the better. Through self-directed growth in body, mind and spirit, they will lead to a greater sense of happiness and feeling at home in the universe.

John White

- John White is Editor of *What is Enlightenment: Exploring the Goal of the Spiritual Path*, author of *The Meeting of Science and Spirit, A Practical Guide to Death and Dying* and the forthcoming *Enlightenment 101: A Guide to God-Realization and Higher Human Culture*. A past Director of Communication for the Institute of Noetic Sciences, John White has published 15 books translated into 10 languages, and his writings have appeared in The New York Times, Reader's Digest, Esquire, Omni, Woman's Day and more.

DEDICATED TO LOVE

*In the mind of the Bodhisattva who dwells depending on deep meditation, there are no obstacles; and, going beyond the perverted views, he reaches final Nirvana. All the Buddhas of the past, present, and future, depending on the deep meditation used, attain to the highest perfect **Enlightenment**.*

The Heart Sutra

This book came about because I am compelled to write about what intrigues me most: the spiritual path to enlightenment. It is intended for anyone who wishes to share my fascination with the enduring wisdom of the ages, and my life-long love affair with Truth in its many guises.

Once, after a weekly 40-minute silent group meditation, I asked a small circle of friends to say in a word what "enlightenment" meant to them. Their thoughtful responses were confirmation that I am on the right track in writing this book, for they spoke so movingly of union, freedom, light, awakened heart. I felt like bowing in deep respect; to my friends, to the guiding impulse that moves this project, and to you, dear reader, for being interested in the Ultimate. Your quest makes this book worth sacrificing the trees it took to create.

The thousands of words that follow are offered only in the spirit of love, for the benefit of all. Remember: they are only markings on paper. *You* give them meaning and power.

Whoever you are, whatever you may believe, however you live, it is my only hope that you find something here that resonates within, and becomes an actual catalyst for your own growth and inevitable Enlightenment.
Honor to the great teachers of all times.

LJB
New Hampshire, 2007

Note: I intentionally use unusual capitalizations for Universe, IT, Self, Truth, Enlightenment, Living Spirit and similar Big words.

3

When the mind sinks into the Self, then the Self is realized. When the mind issues forth, the world appears, and the Self is not realized.

Ramana Maharshi

LIFE'S COSMIC LITTLE SECRETS

*Whatever you think,
it's more than that,
more than that.*

Incredible String Band

Upon purchasing some new computer software, we often find a "Quick Start" section at the beginning of the documentation, for users with some experience (and little spare time), consisting of the refined essentials of the instructions that follow. The assumption is, *if you get the gist of this summation, you can immediately get on with making good use of the program.*

Similarly, the following "Words of Enlightenment" could be seen as the refined distillation of this book (and indeed all the wisdom I've ever been able to acquire). I place these "conclusions" up front because - like William Blake or Rumi, or Dogen,- I believe in the enormous power of a few well-chosen words (while still acknowledging their limitations).

The ideas embodied here could theoretically liberate you instantly, if you are – by whatever definition that is relevant – *ready*. If you truly get the message, congratulations; you are already free, and you may pass the book on to someone else whom you would love to similarly enlighten.

Then again, if these pithy maxims serve to effectively whet your appetite for further exploration, this book is definitely for you, and you are bound to profit from reading on.

Lest my aphorisms strike the reader as too fanciful or poetic for "real life" - and to emphasize the depth of my convictions - I will share with you the fact that as I wrote them, my dear mother, whom I love with all my heart and soul, was dying in the next room, a situation which tended to sharpen my intent and discrimination considerably. If she could but hear and understand, this is the same information I would wish to convey to her, on her way out of this life, as I would to any newborn citizen of this planet, on his or her way in.

Words of Enlightenment

❀ **All Life is ONE.**
Everything is connected and related to everything else.

❀ **All Time is NOW.**
Infinity is HERE. Past, present and future are inseparable.

❀ **Consciousness is Omnipresent and Omniscient**
(everywhere and all-knowing).
Mind creates the world. Matter is frozen light, the original Great Idea.

❀ **Energy Follows Thought.**
We are creating reality and our destiny every moment.

❀ **Creation is Ever-Evolving Pattern.**
Intelligence is universally evident.

❀ **You Are Already Perfect,**
although you may have forgotten this perfection.

❀ **Love is Everything.**
Beauty is everywhere. The mundane is Divine.

❀ **Your Body is a Sacred Gift,** which you gave yourself.
By a trick of attention, you have come to believe that it contains you, but
actually, you contain it.

❀ **Pleasure is No Sin.** In fact, the very intensity and depth of enjoyment
available to you in this body is a kind of brilliant shortcut to the spiritual, and
the redeeming proof of the basic grandness of Existence.

❀ Pain is the greatest teacher, yet
Much of Your Suffering is Unnecessary.

❀ There is nothing to fear. **Death is an Illusion.**
The Universe is your home.
You are never alone.

❀ **It's ALL Right.**
Though you live within unforeseen change and upheaval,
you're still OK. Life is worth the trouble.
Happiness is not only possible, but healthy!

WHAT IS THIS UNIVERSE?

*The philosophy of physics is becoming
indistinguishable from the philosophy of Buddhism,
which is the philosophy of **Enlightenment**.*
- Gary Zukav *The Dancing Wu Li Masters*

We have words for it, yet know It not. We know It exists, yet we know not how. We may refer to It as Creation, Existence, Reality, the Cosmos, Tao, God. We know only a minute fragment of Its body and being; a token of It's limitless properties and possibilities; only a narrow waveband in the stupendously vast spectrum of the Universe.

We feel some of Its energy, but we cannot begin to conceive of Its power. It is so old, so vast, so complex, so spectacular, so minute, so invisible, so subtle, so intelligent, so brutal, so beautiful, that words and numbers, ideas and concepts fail altogether.

So incalculable and miraculous is the Universe that we should be stunned and in awe every morning that we re-awaken to It. So exalted is It, that we should treat even its names with reverence. Do we have even an iota of a chance of understanding It, and our place in this Universe?

DON'T BELIEVE YOUR EYES, UNTIL YOU OPEN THEM

*The earth is a Paradise, the only one we will ever know.
We will realize it the moment we open our eyes. We
don't have to make it a paradise, it is one. We have only
to make ourselves fit to inhabit it.*
Henry Miller

At this very moment, stuck onto a whirling little orb, hooked into an average-looking solar system on the outer spiral of the diaphanous cloud of dusty radiance we call the Milky Way, you are hurtling through space at an unimaginably enormous velocity.

Yet you feel that you are stationary.. that the world is always "under" you; the sky is the very definition of "up." The vaulted exploding heavens appear a motionless canopy. We call this non-sense "common sense."

You look up at the stars and assume that they are all "there" at once, namely "now." Yet each starlight image streaming into your eyes comes from a different time, spanning numerous billions of years. Not only are you literally looking into the past, *but you are actually beholding a multitude of pasts* in one enormous starry vista. Many of the celestial bodies you believe to be "there" are "now" long dead and gone. Our beloved, ever-so-reliable night sky, by which we have navigated for thousands of years, is really an antique apparition. At the same time, since the light of billions of "newer" stars has yet to reach us, there is no way of seeing what's really there!

Even the huge emptiness we behold pervading the cosmos is illusory: astrophysics now tells us it is jam-packed *full* with "dark matter" and "dark energy," and in fact trillions of ghostly particles are shooting right through you all the time.

So, what can we know as "real," and how can we know it?

YOUR BRAIN FILTERS YOUR MIND

Great Knowledge is there before we can do anything. It is already perfect. We do not even need to take up a starting position. We are completely free, from the outset.

Tarthang Tulku

Common misperceptions are caused by the limitations and reality-filtering properties of the brain, which in effect allows you to be someone individual, somewhere specific, and get something done. You sense your body as solid, though you intellectually admit that it is in reality mostly fluid, held in trillions of gelatinous cells, all made of molecules, themselves clever arrangements of atoms which are primarily empty space around energy clouds so ephemeral and transient that brilliant nuclear physicists can only say they have a *tendency* to exist!

Even when the logical, rational scientific intellect proves beyond question that ours is a body of light, we still feel like meat and bones, so persuasive is the testimony of the lying senses.

Then too, I instinctively "know" I am someone specific, definable as distinct from all other instances of sentient awareness there are, or ever were or will exist. Indeed, the most fundamental assumption and basis for all my other beliefs is the unquestionable "fact" of my own individuality. So persuasive is this presumption of the primacy of my identity, that I actually (if secretly) experience myself as the center of the universe.

What is the meaning of these perceptual hoaxes and self-deceptions? Why do we assume that *our* beliefs are the most valuable; that our world is more consequential than all others? Could it be that we fear that the only alternative is to forever feel stupid and small in the face of the infinite?

9

Where does one turn between solipsism (*"I'm IT"*) and the awful realization of our fleeting insignificance in a vast impersonal cosmos ("I'm *nobody*")? How can we find a satisfactory Truth behind the mistakes and mysteries of our lives? The answer is literally and virtually closer than you think.. because it has nothing to do with thought.

BUT FIRST, A QUICK REALITY CHECK

It's the dawn of the Twenty-First Century, and things aren't looking too good: Human civilization is in upheaval; economies are collapsing; nations are in chaos; energy, water and food shortages loom; animal and plant species are going extinct by the thousands; human-caused climate change is accelerating and weather extremes and environmental disasters rage.

Hideous weapons of destruction proliferate worldwide, with no shortage of men willing to use them. "Ethnic cleansing" and suicide terrorism are routine. Cynics and crooks pervade the governments of the world, where guiding morals, ethics and altruistic values seem all but extinct. Massive fraud and corruption reign. Vanity, arrogance and selfishness are the fashion of the day.

Mass media is used by big business to hypnotize and exploit consumers for horrendous profit. Cynical politicians manipulate voters' fears for personal power. While a few self-infatuated financial moguls amass obscene amounts of wealth, millions of innocent people go homeless and starving.

Wholesale disregard for basic civic and cultural values is the norm. Millions rush to willingly abdicate their responsibility and intelligence to smug pundits, bellicose, hateful religious & political fanatics and holy phonies hawking salvation to the ignorant, the small minded, the fearful.

Many American inner-city neighborhoods resemble war zones. Our children's so-called "education" is funded by public gambling.

Cancer ravages three out of four families, while we irradiate and toxify the environment in the name of "jobs," "progress" and "defense." Affordable, quality health care is a cruel myth. Hospitals often make people sicker, prescription drugs kill nearly as often as "cure;" a hundred thousand Americans a year die from medical mistakes and hospital contamination, paying skyrocketing "health care" costs for the privilege.

Overpopulation, pollution, disease, and crime are escalating. What does it mean when the capital city of the "greatest country on earth" ranks highest in alcohol consumption, drug abuse, and murder? Is this nation's crumbling infrastructure a sign that it's soul is equality degenerate? Companies buy and sell "pollution credits," as global warming advances and the ecosystem chokes. Million-year-old forests are systematically annihilated, and thousands of exquisitely unique and beautiful animal, bird, insect, and sea species are driven to extinction, while the fires of deforestation choke off our precious oxygen supply - all to produce and package more poisonous junk "food." Eco-rape continues to be handsomely rewarded, while the earth itself gasps and regurgitates our detritus, and responds with biological menaces, weather extremes and geological catastrophe.

And, as ever - as if we yet lack sufficient lessons from which to learn - the mad, ceaseless killing goes on. We slaughter animals for gluttony, sport and vanity, each other in the name of God or country or "security" or profit.

Everything seems to be getting worse. Are the doomsayers right? Is this The End? If so, what can we do? If not, what can we do?

ULTIMATE QUESTIONS

God has concealed the wind
and shown you the dust.
Rumi

Why all this suffering? Who needs the aggravation? What's the use of trying? Is there a way out? *What's wrong with us?* How could we have degenerated so far? Is this sorry world salvageable? Should we even try, or must we resign ourselves to reaping our just desserts?

Try as we might to push them aside, the eternal cosmic questions continue to haunt us, late at night when sleep won't come.. or when tragedy strikes and shakes up our complacent routine. No matter how sophisticated or busy our lives, that existential itch still demands scratching: *Who am I? Why am I here? What should I do? What's it all about? Is there true wisdom to be found, or is our knowledge limited by our mundane trials? Is happiness possible? At what price?*

Is "reality" really real? And if so, *so what?* Are we doomed to ride the highs and lows of blind fate until the inevitable end, when we take that terrible plunge into the boundless black hole of final extinction?

Consciously or otherwise, your own coping mechanisms lead you to seek or synthesize some explanation for IT ALL, if only to help endure the torments and uncertainties of this earthly existence. However myopic or approximate, your personal working view of life is an attempt to make sense of an impersonal world in an overwhelmingly huge universe. Your attraction to reading these very pages is evidence of this ongoing quest. It has to do with what we could call our greater sense of direction.. the primal, persistent, inner yearning to find our way Home.. to be free.. to be ***Enlightened***.

ROADSIDE RELIGION

God has no religion.
Mahatma Gandhi

All philosophies and world-views - from primitive myths and esoteric cosmologies, to the elusive Unified Field Theory of modern theoretical physics - are attempts at addressing the insistent perpetual conundrum, *What's going on here?* All religions are attempts to record and codify the "answers," and preserve them for posterity. All are partially correct... and potentially misleading.

The Nihilist sees no meaning at all: life is a chronic affliction cured only by death, and nothing matters. Existentialists find life arbitrary, absurd, and full of tragic irony. To fundamentalists, it's all Good and Evil, temptation, sin, punishment, and a possible salvation and reward some time, somewhere else.

Some religions take this life as a kind of proving grounds for aspirants to a better world, with God's holy proxies administering the entrance exams. Thus, we battle earthly enemies for the promise of a perfect paradise hereafter. Vast lexicons of written law evolved to direct our course. On the other hand, some religions hold this world to be an illusion, the dream-play of an omnipotent first cause, citing the impermanence and non-substantiality of all things.

Religions are road maps, recorded by high-minded pioneer visionaries, intent on helping you avoid getting lost. Some of their ancient charts are accurate, some unreliable; some are outdated, some timeless. But please don't confuse the map with the territory.

The gift and genius of religion is that it perpetuates hope and faith, morality and practice. The object of our universal aspiration has been conceived throughout the ages in a variety of ways. Salvation. Godhead. Nirvana. Christ Consciousness, Buddha Mind. Absorption. Illumination. It is not a belief, but rather an experience, a realization, and the point of all religions: Deliverance. Union. Perfection. Grace. Understanding. Wisdom. Ultimately, the Truth of all ways is One, and there is no disagreement anywhere.

The believer is happy,
the doubter is wise.
Greek Proverb

Life is a heroic journey. We are all pilgrims on a great soul-quest, and Enlightenment is the Holy Grail we seek. We can stray, trip up, or get lost, but ultimately and inevitably, every soul must somehow come home to the heart of existence, the realization of Who we really are. Then, seeking ceases, and we perceive a reality we somehow must have known was here all along, but which is startling nonetheless.

Science without religion is lame.
Religion without science is blind.
- Albert Einstein

15

THE MANY NAMES of ENLIGHTENMENT

There must be the cessation of all search, and only then is there a possibility of the coming into being of that which is nameless.

Krishnamurti

Union / Oneness / Non-Duality
Deliverance / Non-Effort
The Alchemical Transformation
Original Perfection
True Nature
The Eye of Wisdom
God Light
Knowing Beyond Knowledge
The Peace That Surpasses All Understanding
Self-Liberating Super-Conscious Insight
The Secret Mystery of Life
The Essence of All Experience
The Absolutely Non-Dependent State
Free Awareness
Eternity / The Deathless
The Endgame of Being
The Living Truth, Unalloyed and Self-Evident

I, ME, MINE

*The self cannot understand Great Space or
Time because it is precisely the embodiment of
a lapse of such understanding.*

Tarthang Tulku

If all this talk of ultimate Enlightenment seems a bit out of reach in light of your daily personal struggles, do not despair. All you have to do is give up your self. ☺

You are not who you think you are, and you have no idea who you really are. You act as if you know yourself. You use the same self-referent first-person pronoun "I" that everyone else does, but believe yourself to be an isolated *someone* with a separate, solid identity.

You identify yourself with your body, your name, your gender, your family and work roles, your religion, your political convictions, your nation. But all of these are costumes created by the unknown Self, so that you might discover another way home through the cosmic maze of creation and re-creation. You are a life-long sightseer who has lost your way, *and then forgotten that you are lost!*

You have been defined by tribal myths, old habits and blind reactions. You have been a happy slave to your inherited truths and tastes, content to live in the fortified crystal palace of your established personality.

You have limited your knowledge of yourself drastically with circumstantial roles, arbitrary allegiances, acquired tastes, fashionable conventions of thought, insatiable desires, overgrown fears, and numerous opinions about what is important or possible. Yet, however elegant and comfortable and perfectly self-justified, your self turns out to be illusory; about as substantial and enduring as clouds.

But in reality, at the same time, YOU are the Creator of IT All.

17

*The lower self does not know that it is asleep;
consequently, what appreciation can it have for
awakening?*

Kabir Helminski

In fact, you are neither your name, nor your social position, nor your job, nor your place within a family, community or nation. Neither are you the body, with which you identify so tenaciously. Only vaguely constant is the physical form, this self-processing conglomeration of cells, tissue, bone and blood.. perpetuated by the devouring of other similarly amorphous formations. Actually, the body is - on successively more accurate "levels" of perception - mostly water, empty space, and pure energy, temporarily and barely bound into the form you so readily identify with.

You are equally misinformed about the outer world. You may think "things" are solid, and that you can possess them, while actually they are ghosts and you are possessed by them. You might believe you know time; space; life.. yet you perceive only their dimmest shadows. This is why we suffer and search. Our sense of self and the world is conceptual, conditioned, and limited. It needs to be experiential, spontaneously trusting, expansive, and all-seeing.

*Recognizing that the true nature of all individuals is
emphatically non-individual, neither lasting nor separate,
is the wisdom of zazen.*
Roger Thomson

To be confused is normal. To be confused and not *know* one is confused is to be deceived indeed. So long as we misidentify with our ideas, positions, and possessions we will need a method to extricate ourselves. In order to become awake, we must practice awakening. Hence the wisdom of meditation. *We sit to see.* "The unexamined life is not worth living."

WISDOM BEYOND WORDS

*It is not outer awareness, It is not inner awareness,
Nor is It suspension of awareness.
It is not knowing, It is not unknowing,
Nor is It knowingness itself.*

*It can neither be seen, nor understood.
It cannot be given boundaries.
It is ineffable and beyond thought.
It is indefinable.
It is known only through becoming It.*

Upanishads

Ironically, the very act of conceptualizing and discussing the illusive gift of enlightenment is fraught with delusion and pitfalls. We over-intellectualized humans are prone to mistaking words for reality - concepts for knowledge - which is dangerous folly. This leads to all sorts of confusion and pain.

Yet there is no stopping the attempt at using this remarkable gift of symbolic language in our quest for understanding and Truth. Our only hope as communicating beings lies in acknowledging the limitations of labels, even as we use them in the attempt to express the ineffable.

Be not deceived. *Enlightenment is not what you think, no matter how much you think about it.* "It" is real, but intangible. It is the most valuable "thing" in the world, but it exists nowhere, and cannot be owned, kept, bought or sold. Its realization is surprisingly simple and utterly profound. It is not an object of striving, but rather an innate state of being which can only be *allowed.* It is closer than your own breath, yet it may take a thousand lifetimes to discover.

Once realized, Enlightenment transforms you completely, though few casual observers may notice any difference at all. It will save your life and release you from it at the same time.

We have two eyes to see two sides of things,
but there must be a third eye
which will see everything at the same time
and yet not see anything.
That is to understand Zen.

D.T. Suzuki

The great teachers spoke of its virtues. Every religion promises it. The mystics sing its praises. Deep down in your heart of hearts, you know it's True. Enlightenment is possible. This very suspicion - hardly justified by our everyday experience - indicates that what we seek is intrinsic, innate, inborn. To look elsewhere amounts to what Ken Wilber calls "wave-jumping in search of wetness." To be enlightened, all you really need is a way to truly know your Self.

ENLIGHTENMENT IN OUR TIME

*If we become alive for a moment, we shall feel that
everything is alive, that all things live, think, feel and
can speak to us.*

P.D. Ouspensky

It's the perennial wisdom. The ancient knowledge. The Single Truth with ten thousand names. Buried and rediscovered yet again, when the hearts of people yearn for the cessation of their needless anguish.

The world is shrinking, and the word is out once more, and - you might say - not a moment too soon. In the soul of a whole new generation of seekers and celebrators; in a wave of enlightening teachers from every culture; in the eyes of wise old souls, and highly evolved newborn messengers; in the pure, channeled wisdom teachings; in the council circles and sweat lodges... It is the source of the sacred in every culture and conviction: the timeless Living Spirit emerges and reveals itself in a new way, on a new day, for a new age: Eclectric.. Iconoclastic. Electronic. Digital. Trans-cultural. Global. Universal.

It is time to spiritualize the pulsing global electromagnetic nerve network of our collective intelligence, and realize our essential Godhead. It's time to become enlightened citizens of an enlightened world civilization. And there's no time to waste, for Mankind and the remaining creatures, and the Earth itself are in immanent peril.

21

Enlightenment is Not...

> *The Enlightened being is no longer faced with the illusion of enlightenment.*
>
> Lex Hixon

Enlightenment is not an achievement. It is not a pot of gold at the end of the rainbow of all our hard work and self-sacrifice. *Enlightenment is the immediate radical realization of your very nature.. unfiltered, absent of delusion and pretense and all mental limitation.* Again, there is nothing you can do about Enlightenment except *be* it. Enlightenment is the original native state and ground of all being. It engenders and includes you, but the "you" with whom you customarily identify cannot not grasp it.

Enlightenment Is Practical.

> *Go beyond the boundary of delusion and enlightenment, and being apart from the paths of the ordinary and sacred, immediately wander freely outside ordinary thinking, enriched with great **enlightenment.***
>
> Eihei Dogen

Christ said we could be as he was, and showed the way. The last words of the Buddha were, *"Work out your own salvation."* The Sufis say you are God playing hide and seek with yourself. There's really nowhere to go but Here.

And there's no time like Now. More than a hopeful ideal, Enlightenment is a real and present option, and it may just save us a world of trouble. It only requires our complete commitment to awakening to the Truth.. about us, nature, the Universe.

Enlightenment Is Radical

Enlightenment is meta-real: It comprises both what you know and what you have yet to conceive, and encompasses all relative levels of reality. It is: Transpersonal. Super-conscious. Omnipresent. Non-temporal. Unpredicted. Non-Conceptual. Non-Dualistic. Boundless. Non-Conforming. Spontaneously Self-Originating. Self-validating, and Deathless.

You Name It, We Need It

Spontaneous Wisdom
Unshakable Knowledge
Conscious Deep Peace,
born of pervasive understanding
of nature's ways.
Universal Insight
Wholeness
Unconditional Equanimity

THE META-HISTORY OF ENLIGHTENMENT

*What we thought obstructed our unity consciousness
never existed in the first place.*
Ken Wilber

The possibility of human beings achieving this exalted state came into the world when evolution produced a brain sophisticated enough to self-reflect: *"Know Thyself."* Christ and Buddha were highly visible examples of the possibilities. But not all fully-realized beings are necessarily known as such, even by their closest associates. Many have mingled in the marketplace unrecognized.

In earlier times there were very few fully evolved souls around. Of necessity, the ways to liberation - and the people who practiced them - were hidden, forced underground or to the fringes of civilization by the very jealousy, intolerance and fear for which they could have been the antidote. Thus, saints became martyrs.

Often the brutal vicissitudes of physical survival left the Light all but extinguished on Earth, except for the occasional private transmission - from master to disciple - of the precious wisdom; otherwise unknown or misunderstood by millions of suffering souls for generations and epochs. Superstitious and afraid, people in those dark ages had no idea how much light was cloistered in monasteries, caves, and the secret hearts of visionaries, shamen, god-intoxicants, wandering mendicants, outcast alchemists, troubadours, poets, clowns, witches and mystics.

Enlightenment has always been an "endangered wisdom." Yet it somehow inevitably re-emerges when necessary. In our times, despite - or perhaps because of - the general breakdown of society, the cumulative influence of Enlightenment on a shrinking planet is growing; a function of our collective need and readiness for a new paradigm of reality and human behavior. Paradoxically, amidst rampant degeneration and unprecedented global disaster, more than ever before in history, opportunities abound for the awakening process to occur. In you. In me. Right here. Right now.

COMING THROUGH

> **Enlightenment** *is never absent. We already <u>are</u> primal awareness. This very mind that is now thinking and reading is none other than Ultimate Consciousness, the Ground of Being.*
>
> Lex Hixon

Occasionally, enlightened mind may come through "channels," personified as separate from the host or hostess; as with Emmanuel, a brilliant and sensitive spiritual teacher who happens to have no physical body, and is channeled through Pat Rodegast. His message in a nutshell: *"Step outside of the shroud of fear, to the excitement and delight of creation."* [1]

Today, there are thousands, and there may soon be millions of fully conscious beings among us. The very survival of the planet requires that the influence of enlightened people everywhere reach a certain critical mass. Won't you help? Your mission, should you decide to accept, is to become enlightened, and save the world.

---

[1] *Emmanuel's Book II The Choice for Love* Compiled by Pat Rodegast and Judith Stanton. Bantam, 1990

SCIENTIFIC MYSTICISM

*Quantum theory has abolished the notion of
fundamentally separated objects, has introduced the
concept of the participator to replace that of the
observer, and has come to see the universe as an
interconnected web of relations whose parts are only
defined through their connections to the whole.*

Firtjof Capra *The Tao of Physics*

Space is literally a food that you are eating.

Tarthang Tulku

In our materialistic civilization, 500 years of rational, analytic reductionism
has prevailed over the metaphysical, supernatural view of the world. Favoring
the testimony of the five human senses, demanding physical evidence, and
unable to quantify the subtle nature of consciousness, our "hard" science has
assumed the convenient/awkward position of ignoring mind altogether.

This practical, if myopic work-around enabled us to deduce much about the
local, obvious, hard bits and pieces of creation, but virtually nothing about the
whole, the unseen, the Creator, the timeless ultimate ground of reality, or even
the human mind itself. Thus the great schism between the physical sciences on
the one hand, and the entire psycho-spiritual landscape of philosophy,
cosmology, religion, poetry and mysticism on the other.

The material paradigm functioned satisfactorily until we began to confuse our
physical view of the world with all of reality. The infatuation with "things," and
our pride in our mastery over them eventually led to a false sense of superiority
over nature, and a dangerous attitude of domination and control. The errors of
this approach are evident in man-made environmental disasters, as well as the
spiritual emptiness felt by so many people.

Fortunately, everything is about to change. Because the world is one, both the
inner and outer sciences - the Eastern and Western pursuits of truth - had to
eventually reach the same conclusions. This is the historic moment when
disparate world views merge, commencing the healing of the great rift in the
human psyche between the heart and the head.

METTA-PHYSICS

Modern physics posits a *quantumized* view of creation, in which unfathomable quantities of sub-atomic concentrations of light-speed energy generate matter *by their tendency to exist or not*, in and out of the present space/time continuum.

Ancient Buddhism speaks of the smallest possible discrete unit of time (*astakalapa*). All of manifested creation is said to be repeatedly "projected" and "un-projected" within this unimaginably finite period. The resulting blur from this hyper-speedy oscillation is what we usually perceive as "reality." Enlightenment entails the direct perception of the mind-moments between world-projections. Nirvana - the timeless, unmanifest state of pure awareness - fully permeates and inter-exists within samsara, the illusion of concrete "reality" full of "things" "out there."

The astonishing results of their own investigations into the extremely small, the enormously distant, and the impossibly fast have forced the quantum physicists to agree with the mystics: that existence is one seamless whole; that time and space are as relative as matter and energy; that the Universe is multidimensional yet completely interconnected, and the underlying determinant of all creation and experience is quite literally *in your mind*.

We already see the applications of this paradigm shift in the new fields of mind/body medicine such as psychoneuroimmunology, biofeedback, and spiritual healing. In just a few short years, the cutting edge in healing has gone from high-tech chemical intervention to organic auto-regulation.

At the same time that science is becoming "mystical," the yogis and gurus have been compelled by the spread of civilization and communication to leave their high hermitages for the marketplace of ideas, to demystify their knowledge for a ready world, and apply the wisdom of the ages to the practical problems of the planet. Could this be the true Age of Enlightenment?

ELUSIVE LIGHT EVERYWHERE

*Gaining **enlightenment** is*
Like the moon reflecting in the water.
The moon does not get wet, nor is the water disturbed.
Although its light is extensive and great...
The whole moon and whole sky are reflected
in a dew-drop in the grass, in one drop of water.
Enlightenment does not disturb the person,
just as the moon does not disturb the water.
A person does not hinder enlightenment,
just as a dew-drop does not hinder the moon in the sky.
The depth of the drop is the height of the moon.

Eihei Dogen

Fish can't see water.

Elam

Enlightenment, like love, cannot be installed in you by someone else, yet it helps to be around the loving, *and* the enlightened. The illumination process may be slow and subtle, like the ripening of summer fruit, or it may be sudden and definite as a bubble bursting. You are never quite the same, and yet you have only become what you always truly were.

To be free we must be comfortable in being someone,
anyone, or no one, at any time in any place.
Each morning, if we commit ourselves to finding the
Truth of every situation, then miracles will come to us all
day long.

Sujata

Enlightenment wears a million faces, yet its authenticity is self-revealing and startling. Find it when and where you are: in the presence of a laughing child; in a mother's gesture of unconditional love; in the wink of an eye from a strange old man offering a bit of wise advice with the direct force of spiritual truth; from a passage in one of those holy books that finds you when you are ready; on the World Wide Web; in the awakening realization of the stunning beauty and perfection of nature; In your lover's eyes and body. At the moment of your death.

> *An indescribable peace.. a "diamond moment of reality,"*
> *came flowing into (or indeed, waking up within) me, and I*
> *realized that all around me everything was lit with a kind*
> *of inner shining beauty.*
> The Common Experience

BARKING UP THE RIGHT TREE

Life is a kind of glorious nonsense.

Alan Watts

There is no way to Truth.
Truth is the way.

Mahatma Gandhi

Everyone is looking for personal happiness. Whatever you are doing, ultimately it is in order to be happy. Why do we work? To make money. For what? To buy protection and possessions. To what end? To be able to cease our toiling and be comfortable; safe; secure. Or to be entertained, even thrilled.

Most "happiness" is relative, conditional, a short-lived satisfaction leaving us in need of more of whatever we desire. Indeed, circumstantial security is an illusion in a world of ceaseless change. As long as we believe it comes from something out there, satisfaction and contentment elude us.

What is your own definition of happiness? What do you really want for yourself? Examine your desires and motivations thoroughly enough and you will find that each *condition* is only for the purpose of gaining another.

Enlightenment knows that reliance on circumstances is futile and that the ultimate happiness is wanting nothing. "Want" implies lack. Enlightenment is understanding that you lack nothing - that it's really *all right..* as is.. immediately, always, and forever.

Even while we spend our days trying to solve the next problem, in the hopes of attaining that which we think we need, Enlightenment resides in the deeper, non-dependent, non-striving peace, *in the very midst of problems and problem solving:* Effortless effort. Nirvana-in-Samsara (Union within the illusion of separateness). Eternity in the moment.

Not merely part of creation,
You are creator of your part.

- Nadar

Among the great mystics, those who spoke at all left essentially the same message: The very essence of creation and experience is only here and now, the Kingdom of Heaven within. Or as Tim Leary paraphrased it so "psyche-delicately," *all of galactic time has labored to produce this moment.* If not here, where? If not now, when?

*Setting **Enlightenment** as our goal*
ensures that we won't get it

Wes Nisker

The open secret - the radical truth - is that real happiness is universally available, constant and everlasting, independent of situation or predicament. Once we realize this, such unconditional contentment becomes the only really worthwhile pursuit. Yet paradoxically, *pursuing precludes attainment!* If the truth be known, there is really nothing to do but awaken to the realization of your own infinite Self-nature. Enlightenment isn't something you get, it's what you *are.*

The danger of course, upon hearing such a proclamation, is that the self-invested ego will appropriate the notion for its own aggrandizement. But the moment someone claims Enlightenment, *that's not it at all!* Enlightenment and ego are mutually exclusive (or at least inversely proportional): *It is absolutely impossible to assert with any validity that "I am enlightened," not because the "enlightened" part is false, but because the "I" part is false.*

The burden of responsibility for creating my life had been lifted from me by the assurance that life creates itself.

Eric Lerner

31

SOME CALL IT BLISS.

I have been in that heaven the most illumined
By light from Him, and seen things which to utter
He who returns hath neither skill nor knowledge;
For as it nears the object of its yearning
Our intellect is overwhelmed so deeply
It can never retrace the path that it followed.
But whatsoever of the holy kingdom
Was in the power of memory to treasure
Will be my theme until the song is ended.

Dante *Inferno*

Enlightenment is not to be confused with self-absorbed apathy. In a perfect Universe, it's still a relatively imperfect world, and there's plenty of work to be done. Enlightenment does not eliminate our problems, although it places them in a refreshing perspective. In fact, it makes everyone else's problems your own. Yet that is no problem either.

One appears to strive, but no friction is generated. Thus the wonderful paradox of *non-desperate urgency.* It is the magical union of the wisdom which perceives the perfect illusion, and the compassion which acts full-time to relieve real suffering, improve the world and optimize the possible.

In other words, once you glimpse the exquisite timeless cosmic order of things - the absolute inevitability and perfect timing of all situations - you still act in earnest, in Love, to help people, generally make a positive difference. We can be deadly serious, with humor. Seeing heaven is the conception of Enlightenment. The intent to bring it to earth is its birth.

Soul is not in the universe, but the universe is in it.

Plotinus

DO IT NOW

That which is most elusive must, of course
be the very thing to be pursued.
Listen to the farthest sound.

Jesse Pollack

Jesus saith, Let not him who seeks, cease until he finds;
And when he finds, he shall be astonished;
Astonished he shall reach the Kingdom,
And having reached the Kingdom, he shall rest.

Oxyrhynchus Papyrus

Enlightenment used to be a purely reclusive pursuit, but the 21st Century version is - must be - thoroughly immersed in "real life." Whether you're involved in parenting or politics or the performing arts, business or beachcombing, as the great yogi saint Ramana Maharshi said, *There is no conflict between work and wisdom.*

In times past, Enlightenment was embodied and perpetuated by remote rabbi's, lone yogis, mystical clans, monastic brotherhoods. Today we have all forms, plus the form of no form. Superconsciousness is where you find it, and where you put it. The uncompromising passion for Truth recognizes and engenders Truth, no matter where or when, in shape or out.

Nothing is excluded on this path, for where could Ultimate Reality possibly *not be?* Opportunity - to test your insights and practice what you preach, to see the hidden become obvious - will be everywhere. In your mailbox; on TV; in cyberspace; with your crazy kids; in your sexuality; in the very fear of death. In the decay of cities and the renewal of nature. Everything that "sticks" shows where you have to let go. You'll have to consecrate your desires and dedicate your emotions to Enlightenment. All enemies become the guru in drag. Obstacles magically transform themselves into teachings. Darkness is illuminated by enlightened view.

*Do not sit and wait for enlightenment,
for great **enlightenment** is to be found in
everyday activities such as eating, or drinking tea*

Eihei Dogen

Be Ready. Inspiration, instruction and evidence can come through a lyrical poem, a creative music video, or a gift from your mother-in-law. Ultimate understanding can be concealed or revealed in all beings. Who have you overlooked? Our predispositions can blind or reveal. I may look like I'm going downtown for a newspaper, but actually, I'm going to get enlightened.

Good Luck! The only way out is through. Take heart. *"Yea, though I walk through the valley of the shadow of death, I will fear no evil."* Every turn holds the possibility to see The Way.. Reality, which is Creation in action. Rejoice at the chance!

*You must totally participate in the miracle of what is,
right now, right here. That is All.*

Nadar

WHAT IS SPIRITUAL?

Spirituality is revealed in how you treat the next person you meet. Transcending assumed limitations is the first step towards feeling your connection to the Universe. Pursuing a vision is an expression of faith in that connection. Communing with Nature is another universal spiritual experience, and protecting the environment has become a holy act.

Many indigenous cultures in the Americas, Australia, the South Pacific, and the Orient never have distinguished the spiritual from the mundane. Not only are we all one people, but we are All One Life. There is only one Creation, and we are IT. When we realize this universality, *everything is sacred*, everyone is precious, and - mysteriously - we seem to require less effort to get along.

TO HEAL THE SOUL

In recent years, greater numbers of people are embracing the holistic view of health - which includes the "soul" or "spirit" as well as the body and mind. Though this is the most subtle and elusive human dimension to discuss, it is the underlying determinant of one's entire condition. Veteran physicians know that the chances of physical recovery are considerably reduced when a patient is "spiritually sick." Such issues as hope and despair, connectedness and isolation, joy and grief become critical variables when our health hangs in the balance. These soul-level factors may constitute the root cause and ultimate cure of disease. A skilled psycho-spiritual healer can discern a person's fears, beliefs and aspirations, as well as their physical symptoms. The process of self-inquiry is therapeutic, and it helps reveal the attitudes, awareness, and self-image which in turn affect behavior and ultimately, one's health and well being.

WHAT ABOUT PAIN?

*Only part of the equation
is what's happening.
More important is
your response to It All.*
Nadar

Pain is a necessary aspect of life and growth. Buddhism's First Noble Truth is the inevitability of suffering. Bodily pain is the rude reminder of the price we pay for individual incarnation - the confinement of omni-consciousness in a local, vulnerable, aging package of biological tissue - just as bodily pleasure is the reward for doing it anyway.

Years ago, I read in *Voluntary Controls* (by the Western yogi Jack Schwarz), that anyone could - as he had learned to - push steel needles through their skin without feeling pain or bleeding. I believed him.

Once, to test the yogic mind/body exercises I had been studying, I requested that my dentist use no anesthesia for a root-canal operation I was in for. Essentially, I wanted to see if I could transcend the pain of direct drilling on raw nerve inside my head through mind control alone. More than skeptical, but intrigued, Dr. Miner consented, provided we could keep a hypodermic needle ready and loaded with Novocaine.

We didn't need it. My practice held. In the half-hour root canal operation, including the destruction of the infected nerve, I rarely flinched, and required no anesthesia or drugs. My blood pressure and respiration rate were below normal throughout the procedure. The dentist and his assistant were quite surprised, but I wasn't.

To achieve this internal pain control, I used very deep relaxation and breathing exercises, and two different mental techniques: *high focus* and *complete diffusion*. They seem like opposites, but both rely on the potentially boundless power of conscious attention.

High focus on pain involves the objective, insight into it's transience. It sounds impossible, but even intense pain can be completely accepted when "seen through" as totally impermanent. Of course this is only possible if the witness is mentally free.. that is, one has mastered *objective forbearance*. In deep meditation, pain can be thoroughly experienced, without identification or reaction.

The seemingly opposite approach to acute pain, complete diffusion, expands awareness beyond its site and source, to include the rest of the (painless) body, and beyond. In this instance, extreme disassociation with the body leads to a much wider world view, also known as *astral projection.*

In such "out-of-body" experiences, the pain still exists, but it is perceived within an extremely wider context: in it's full realization, that of all time and space. In effect, conscious union with the infinite beyond is a pretty effective pain killer! The science of psychoneuroimmunology explains this by observing the opiod endorphins secreted in the brain during episodes of euphoria. Subjectively, we are fully experiencing our healing connection with the ground of all being and tapping just a teeny bit more of it's boundless energy.

I do not recommend undergoing unanesthetized surgery without prior meditation practice, but like Mr. Schwarz, I can say that anyone is capable of such mind-over-body mastery. My dental pain control experience proved for me that mind yoga is not a trick, but a science: replicable and democratic. Like First Aid, it belongs to everybody and it helps to know in emergencies.

High Focus
The most enlightened means of dealing with necessary physical pain is not to fight it, but to perceive its finiteness and impermanence. When you're in pain, your pain is real, and important. Don't recoil or try to escape. Don't hide or mask your pain. Relax, release, open to the pain's very nature: its size, shape, intensity, and specific characteristics. Vocalize freely, literally sounding out the pain. Then make room for this *localized* pain in your *greater* awareness.

Complete Diffusion
Recognize the smallness of "your" pain amidst everyone else's, and within the vastness of all the space in the Universe where it is not. Big Mind is the antidote to your separate suffering. Realize that everything changes. And keep breathing.
Meditation can help significantly when dealing with pain, which otherwise so readily leads to exhaustion and depression. Between the extremes of despair and elation, remain centered. Use mantra and prayer to mirror the incredible placebo power of your mind.

Psychological and emotional pain are even more difficult, dangerous and common than the physical variety. Mental anguish is easier to fall into, and more difficult to transcend, for we are often more attached to our beliefs and personal drama than even to our bodies. We detach from our bodies when we fantasize, dream, sleep, or get drunk, but rarely do we loosen the bonds of the ego's emotional story-line, which is actually the root of most of our suffering.

Even Pain Is A Type Of Light

Suffering and pain are unavoidable, but not unworkable. On this path, difficulty inevitably enlarges one's view. You contain what is necessary by realizing your greater nature.

Pain is only increased by "holding on." We usually compound the problem by *suffering about our suffering*. Practice letting go of everything you can think of, even "your" pain. Even wounded animals are noble, not dramatic.

To escape the prison of small mind, you must radically transform your point of view. *Take the pain, the fear, the depression, and dedicate it to the very liberation of all other living beings.* Take comfort in the knowledge that no one else is feeling your pain; that there are in fact millions of people experiencing happiness and peace at this very moment. In this most selfless gesture, miraculously, pain opens your heart to all sentient beings that are suffering, or have suffered. The walls of isolation suddenly crumble, and you are free of suffering, not because it is gone, but because *the sufferer no longer exists.*

SPIRITUAL HEALING EXERCISES

1) <u>Look within</u>. Literally, in a mirror, gaze deeply into your own eyes for several minutes, seeing all of yourself, including your pain, your potential, and your wisdom. Keep looking. Speak to yourself, with forgiveness, appreciation and encouragement. Look into the depths of your own soul. If you think that the person you are looking at is not a child of God, look again.

2) <u>Give thanks</u>. Count your blessings. Share them with those less fortunate. Everyday is Thanksgiving.

3) <u>Use affirmations</u>. Think positively. *I am the Living Spirit of the Universe in the eternal now; Let there be Light*, or *God be my Guide*.

4) <u>Read words of inspiration</u>. Select your mental diet wisely. Please don't waste your precious, fleeting time on this earth with meaningless banter, sensationalism and gratuitous hyper-stimulation. Let the Masters of the Ages influence you for the better.

5) <u>Play</u>. Though it can be conditioned out of us, children and even animals show us how instinctive playfulness really is and it helps to be around them. Humor, games, sports, dance, music and art all restore this sense of spontaneous joy. Express it in the beauty of your home. Compose poetry. Make love.

6) <u>Cultivate intuition</u>. Listen for enlightening messages from your subconscious and superconscious. Look for uncanny coincidences. Keep a dream journal. Trust to your gut feelings. Follow your hunches and instincts. Ask for signs and verify them with a phone call. Consult your heart.

7) <u>Participate</u>. No person is an island. Share with your neighbors. Celebrate holidays and milestones. Discover your sense of community, history and civic pride. Help those in need. Participate in academic traditions, tribal rites timeless customs and global efforts.

8) <u>Heal an old wound</u>. Forgive adversaries. Think kind thoughts. Send an apology. Practice random acts of kindness. Pay it Forward.

9) <u>Meditate</u>. Allow the mind to be quiet. Be in the present. Open to the richness of the moment. Listen. What is your body telling you?

10) <u>Pray</u>. Take a retreat. Commune with the Source of Life. Surrender your worries and recharge your spiritual batteries.

When it comes to soul healing, a little light dispels a lot of darkness. Find spiritual nourishment wherever you can, then make the most of it. With faith and determination, you may rediscover that first and best medicine, inner peace.

THE ABSOLUTE POWER OF MIND

*It is the enlightened mind
which arouses the thought of **enlightenment***

Eihei Dogen

*The existence and the non-existence of the external
world are recognized as rising from the mind itself*

Lankavatara Sutra

Be careful what you want, for you will get it. *"Energy follows thought"* is a cardinal principle in esoteric science. Just to grasp the implications of this is awesome and humbling. We finally perceive how absolutely crucial and potent every thought we entertain is. *Thought is the root of action, which creates the leaves of karma, and the fruit of destiny.* When thoughts become words they have tremendous power to heal or wound. Guard your thoughts as if your world depended on it. It does. The key to right thought is right intention.

*By thinking in terms of Light, you add Light to that
already existing*

The Findhorn Plant Devas

One's mind is the first (and often the only) thing he or she can readily change. Our individual thoughts constantly re-create our inner and outer world, including – ultimately - our states of health and wealth, our relationships, our life's work, and our soul's evolution.

Individual mind power influences the world at large because our "private" minds are actually local aspects of Big Mind, which permeates the Universe as both Creator and Creation, and connects everything with everything else. Our relative "reality" is a projection of our consensus of perceptions at the moment. Buckminster Fuller defined Universe as the sum total of all experience of all consciousness in all time. The Big Bang was the original great idea, and creation is it's manifestation. Realizing this confers Godliness, and general good luck.

*I suddenly became thoroughly **enlightened** and realized
that all things in the universe are mind-essence itself*

Sixth Zen Patriarch

Thoughts have form (visible to practiced clairvoyants), and - deliberate or unconscious - they impart tangible impact in the world. Thoughts can be used as tools, medicines, or weapons. Directed mind power can accomplish almost anything conceivable. World-class athletes practice mental success rehearsal. Of course conscious living is the ultimate sport.

*You are what you think until you stop thinking.*Finally discovering the immense potency of thoughts obliges us to take responsibility for them, which is of course, easier said than done. Our mental habits - often inhibiting and destructive - took a lifetime to develop, and may take a while (and energy) to change.

You may look in the mirror and believe you know who you are seeing; yet only see your projections and expectations. *What you "see" is what you get.* You get up in the morning and assume a habitual identity that precludes an infinite variety of experience and insight. To perceive the world clearly and become who you really are requires nothing less than "dying" and being reborn daily, indeed every moment.

There are many methods, but all depend upon *right intention.* Meditation stills the habitual mind, fosters insight, and enlarges perception of Great Mind. Mantra - the repetition of sacred sounds - focuses the mind one-pointedly. Prayer opens and guides the heart.

Biofeedback technology confirms that every thought has physiological effects, which explains why just visualizing a naturally soothing and healing environment is effective for reducing stress. Medical patients now routinely lower blood pressure, abate migraine headaches, stimulate immunity, and accelerate healing through mind-based techniques. It tuns out that all systems in the organism and each of its trillions of cells is accessible through conscious mental action. The key ingredients are right motivation, imagination, and will-power.

SYMPTOMS OF ENLIGHTENMENT

Three kinds of transcendent emotion radiate from
Enlightenment: *compassion, gratitude, and laughter.*
Each is without object or subject and is marked by
spontaneity.

Lex Hixon

Light does not shine toward itself, and enlightenment is anonymous. It sports no medals. Like a perfect mirror, it is invisible, yet in it we see ourselves. It is born of solitude, yet it serves all life tirelessly. It is fearless, gracious, astute, funny, spontaneous, compassionate.. and sometimes also sad, from perceiving the mass of unnecessary suffering in the world.

The determined seeker who escapes the cave of suffering and illusion to bask in the awesome brilliance of Truth does not worry. Such enlightened people enjoy the admiration of children, the affection of animals, and the respect of open-hearted souls everywhere. They sleep well, laugh easily, and are not afraid of death. Enlightenment involves all senses and awareness in the fullest possible experience of Reality, on all levels. It is not necessarily knowing all there is to know, but rather seeing how it all fits.

SERENDIPITY: WHEN YOU LEAST EXPECT IT.

*It is this very moment
that is most precious.*

Nyaponika Thera

Sudden Enlightenment may visit in ephemeral glimpses of non-ordinary reality, (*satori* in Zen), and what Annie Besant termed "eruptions of the super-conscious." We may prepare for this, but not predict it, for it comes as a stroke of Grace, out of time, and may just as suddenly vanish.

You may have already had - and discounted or forgotten - moments of enlightenment - those "peak experiences" when the ordinary is revealed as extraordinary, and you see way beyond what you thought reality was. In that early childhood out-of-body occurrence; or upon hearing a Beethoven symphony; during an unbelievably exquisite orgasm; or in some pre-dawn epiphany that you would later misinterpret as a fantastic dream. For a moment, "you" dissolved into It All, and became The One.

A glimpse may come in the "second wind" of athletic competition, or the transcendence induced by religious ritual, or in an undeniably "true dream." Or from fasting, extreme stress, near death experience, or psychedelic sacraments. The revelation is as memorable and undeniable as it is indescribable. It is the sublime taste of meta-physical reality that forevermore flavors your everyday life. Enlightened Mind - intuitive, cosmic clarity -.may shine through in moments of crisis or life-threatening emergencies: Your parachute won't open.. You could get enlightened on the way down.

Perhaps for a moment you are infused with heavenly light. You behold incredible beauty everywhere. You stand in awe on the threshold of Infinity and perceive all of Creation with the timeless vision of the mystics. The last traces of doubt and apprehension evaporate in the absolute realization of the Universal One/None.

43

*There was once a Zen master who said that his first
Satori experience consisted of recognizing all people
as himself. Everybody he met had his own face.*
Janwillem Van de Wetering

If we are lucky, the effects of such an epiphany - our Enlightenment moment - lingers.. in our perceptions, attitudes, intentions. Even the memory of Enlightenment can enlighten.

But Enlightenment has no handle to grasp, no number to redial. Enlightenment is a whimsical lover, to embrace and let go. It confers no credentials, and there is no guaranteed membership. Which is why meditation is prescribed: to anchor the precious insight into the rest of life. Meditative practices are not for creating Enlightenment, but for rendering us more likely to recognize and *re-member* it. You become the skilled host to an honored guest.

If you are very set in your ways - too invested in "normality" to consciously contain the Eternal - then the judging intellect inevitably overrides the experience.. evaluating, interpreting, doubting and rationalizing the episode; explaining it away, parking it somewhere "sensible," in its place within the context of your everyday struggle to survive. You may even deny that the experience had any value or significance at all. Such is the cleverness and tenacity of the petty ego-mind, that it soon convinces us that we are not enlightened, that God is not immanent, and that The Kingdom of Heaven is not in fact within.

*Now that he holds it
he knows this treasure
above all others:
Faith so certain
shall never be shaken
by heaviest sorrow*
Bhagavad Gita

BE AS CHILDREN

You don't have to rehearse to be yourself.

Stewart Emary

How can Enlightenment be cultivated in an age of deception, greed, hatred, distraction and info-glut? Where can The Living Truth be discovered in a cynical and shallow pop-culture, immersed in desire and obsessed with material power? Can Enlightenment be transmitted in school?.. in a book?.. in church?.. on TV or the Web? In a dream?

A tidal wave of spirit is moving across the subconscious landscape, and emerging in every region and human community. Could this be IT? How may I best become receptive and participate?

*The attainment of enlightenment from
ego's point of view is extreme death.*

Chogyam Trungpa

Our everyday knowledge comes from a language-base of complex, learned facts, composed of all information ever received. But MIND is much bigger and deeper than what we merely remember and retain. Consciousness contains - but is not defined by - the sum total of all experience, knowledge, ideas, memories, instincts, and perceptions, including the subconscious and super-conscious, proprioceptive and genetic. Unbound awareness *engenders* every thing.

Imagine the intrinsic experience of eliminating all interpretive filters, ceasing all evaluation and categorizing. Imagine the mind of the newborn: Language-free, non-comparing, non-judging, non-self-referent, non-formed, non-delineated. Enlightened.

*Be empty, that is all.
The Perfect Man uses his mind like a mirror -
going after nothing.*

Master Chuang

45

ORIGINAL AWARENESS /
TRANSPERSONAL REALITY

> *The superabundant overflow*
> *of the One*
> *is still simply the One*
>
> — Lex Hixon

> *Though you tie a hundred knots,*
> *the string remains one.*
>
> Rumi

Penetrating understanding arises from our deep, original nature. The brain and its morphogenic extension, the body, have obfuscated the true view, but IT is right here all along, in your own latent ability to perceive all possible awareness, with or without form.

All the best advice is not about what to think, but how to *see,* and be. It's up to you, and it comes *from* you. *The living paradox is that everything in your known universe is both outside your body and inside your mind.*

> *Where else is the very Life*
> *of the Universe*
> *but right here,*
> *rushing through us,*
> *beating our hearts,*
> *breathing our breaths,*
> *knowing our knowledge.*
>
> Nadar

Original Awareness has no indigenous culture, no agenda or destination. To the completely opened mind, the "meaning" of life is nothing other than the full real-time experience itself. The challenge of Enlightenment is to realize that you are God, without forgetting that everyone else is too.

> *I know nothing else but miracles*
> Walt Whitman

What you seek is within. We are talking about the primacy of mind in all experience. To discover how to use your head to liberate your body and soul, please meditate. Be mindful, kind, and patient. Be positive. Be generous of spirit, and guard your thoughts. Use your best intention to enhance your overriding purpose. Be ready for Enlightenment always and in this very moment, and never deny the potential.

> *May the Real Light shine*
> *on me this day..*
> *May the Real Me see it.*
>
> Elam

When you look into the eyes of an enlightened being, your life is forever changed. When that being addresses you, informs you of what you can do for your own Enlightenment... well, you would be a fool not to take heed. In fact *Enlightenment resides within the very attitude of readiness itself.* Even now, it co-exists within your everyday, busy, doubtful, troubled mind, veiled for the most part by the adopted mind-set of all your other assumed concerns. The "separate" unenlightened personality is a complex, brilliant deception, created by and within enlightened mind. (Your mother never told you this?!)

> *If you don't believe in miracles,*
> *you don't know yourself.*
>
> Nadar

47

Lonny J. Brown

CRAZY WISDOM STRIKES AGAIN

*Freedom is understanding we are not in control and
never will be...
the secret to life is "letting go
with all your might."*

Wes "Scoop" Nisker, *Crazy Wisdom*

Crazy Wisdom - AKA "Divine Madness " - is Enlightenment as manifested
by certain highly original characters who fit in no categories and break all the
rules. Crazy Wisdom is ironic, humorous, wild, contradictory. It is the
spontaneous free-spirited, teachings of those masters of life who we usually
recognize too late as truly inspired. Frequently ignored or barely tolerated in
their own times, they're the visionary rebels, the nonconforming creative artists
of the soul, the cultural conscientious objectors who challenge and chide us
when we take ourselves too seriously.

Notable examples of the crazy wise include the Indian saint, Neem Karoli
Baba, who wore only a blanket and would often disappear when too many
devotees gathered; the renegade Tibetan monk Trogyam Trungpa Rinpoche,
who imbibed generous amounts of saki while nearly single-handedly
transplanting Tibetan Buddhism to the West; and the great thirteenth-century
Islamic poet, Rumi, who exhorted his readers to "behead yourself."

Crazy wisdom is the antidote for self-righteousness, religiosity, and spiritual
chauvinism. It is the pro-nonsense path of psychic survival in an insane world.
Crazy wisdom is the ultimate coping skill that masters life's uncertainties and
contradictions by embracing them. It takes into account the awesome vastness of
the universe, and the all-too predictable stupidity of humans.

At once secular and super-natural, beyond logic and reason, crazy wisdom can
come through prayer, meditation, dreams, nature, art, wine, hallucinogens,
ecstatic dance, poetry and song, but rarely in organized churches and schools. It
can be playful, contrary, innocent, romantic, idealistic, iconoclastic or downright
anti-establishmentarian. It is ever-changing, but always authentic. Watch for
Crazy Wisdom at a spontaneous happening near you.

THE FOREST & THE TREES: TRANSCENDING DUALITY

A tree gives glory to God
by being a tree.
Thomas Merton

Our common mental habit of perceiving the world dualistically - in terms of separation and difference - is so all-pervasive that we neither recognize it nor entertain even the possibility that dualism is not "real."

Nevertheless, whatever boundary we see that separates, also co-defines the opposites. Carefully examine anything in the world (or the cosmos) and the distinction between this and that, "here" and "there" proves arbitrary, as does that between now and then, mind and body, man and nature, the microcosmic and microcosmic, or ultimately, between you and me.

Esteemed world-class theoretical physicists echo the ancient Buddhist view of co-arising interdependence: that every "local" event is simultaneously mutually reflecting all others everywhere else. In other words, *there's just no such thing as things.*

This enlightening insight spontaneously occurs like a shift in perception, from figure to ground, from focus to overview. "Giving up Duality" is not changing behavior, but rather changing perception. It leads to tremendous psychological and spiritual breakthrough. The idea is to find the kinship in the differences, the whole in the parts, the macrocosm in the microcosm. This insight goes beyond seeing commonality among many.. it is perceiving their very *unity.*

Unify

Masculine / Feminine
Within / Without
Self / Other
Good / Bad
Past / Future
Us / Them
Heaven / Earth
Mundane / Spiritual
Matter / Energy
Illusion / Enlightenment

THE SELF & ITS DISAPPEARANCE

*The whole premise of individuality is an illusion. There is
no individual to be liberated. There is only one being,
one universal consciousness which is temporarily
expressing itself through all of these forms.*

Robert Najemy

To go beyond yourself, you must know yourself.

Sri Nisargadatta Maharaj

It is by the One that all beings are beings.

Plotinus

The supreme irony of the separate ego is that the construct upon which is
based our whole identity and effort is an imaginary phantom.

Of course, on a relative level, it is true that you are some-*one*, and well you
should be. Contrary to beliefs common among the haircloth set, you don't have
to do violence to the ego to advance spiritually. A positive appreciation of one's
personhood is more than permissible, it is essential. We have to develop a
healthy, well-integrated sense of self before we can transcend it. Just don't take
your "self" so seriously! Your personality is a tool, no less than your hand is.
There's no need to cut it off to be "free."

But when we see through our own particular personality - into the
transpersonal and universal - we learn that "I" am not finite or solid or separate.
Depending on what lengths you've gone to promote or defend your "self," this
may be seen as startling, funny or tragic, but nevertheless, the radical truth is
that you have been investing in a fraudulent account, called "Me."

Upon hearing such identity-threatening pronouncements, newcomers to the
transcendental quest are often perplexed, even annoyed. No matter.. that too is
the predictable reaction of the petulant ego. ☺

*Instead of setting about saying there is a mind, or an
ego, and I want to kill it, you must begin to seek its
source and find that it does not exist at all.*

- Ramana Maharshi

51

There are ways of breaking through the illusion of the little self, some of which are described in this book. Traditional methods generally involve a process of purification: pruning back the over-growth of self-centeredness: arrogance, greed, fear, glamour, pride.. Monasticism evolved in support of this behavioral approach.

The more radical, direct method cuts to the root of the problem through meditative investigation and insight into the non-substantiality of the separate identity. There's no need to fight the ghost when it dissolves in the light of unwavering intelligent scrutiny.

> *Give up owning things and being somebody.*
> *Quit existing*
>
> Rumi

Of course, paradoxically, it is precisely the small self that now wishes to win this new prize, Enlightenment.. and inevitably for all the wrong reasons. Approaching Enlightenment as just another personal achievement is just spiritual greed. In this game, the "ego incognito" can be quite clever and subtle, perpetuating itself by masquerading as the truth-seeker, replete with high spiritual principles, assuming false modesty. Even unworthiness is an ego trip. Maddening, isn't it? *How in the world can one want to not want?*

> *The apparent emptiness of simple presence*
> *is richer than the crowded experience*
> *of ordinary personality.*
>
> Kabir Helminski

> *When all the ways of being a self are let go and when*
> *all phenomena are seen to be empty, then all the*
> *ways of describing this have also vanished."*
>
> Sutta Nipata

UNITY AWARENESS

You needn't try to destroy the separate self, because it isn't there in the first place. All you really have to do is look for it, and you won't find it. That very not-finding is itself an acknowledgment of unity consciousness.

Ken Wilber

The flip-side of ego-transcendence is cosmic consciousness. It's the pay-off for your act of faith in ceasing the struggle to prevail. You discover to your great astonishment that life automatically and perpetually goes on through you, without any effort whatsoever, for you are none other than the very livingness of the universe. This may sound pretty far-out, but notice how you secretly wish and hope it's all true. It is.

If you want to realize the unconstructed nature beyond concepts, resolve your own mind and rest in naked awareness.

Tilopa

Ultimately, the dichotomy between subject and object is a false one; any sense of separation between you and the entirety of the universe is actually imaginary, albeit functional within the everyday world of life in time and space. When you realize this, everyone you confront becomes the Self in disguise. Furthermore (blasphemy warning..) there's no difference between sacred and profane.. it all depends on where you're coming from. You are instantly purified by your highest intentions.

Finally understanding the abiding fundamental fact of unity-in-multiplicity, every experience and contact automatically unites and enlightens. There is no longer any local source of truth. Everyone is the guru, and there are no enemies. There is only the ALL.. being us. (As HH the Dalai Lama so often says, your worst enemy is your greatest teacher.)

Does all this universality mean that personal privacy, making money, brushing your teeth or opposing crime are unenlightened? Hardly. It means that with increasing realization, one's actions come not from desperation and fear, but from wisdom, harmony and humor. You may still work hard at the very same job, yet from a much more spacious perspective. Enlightenment can be at once fierce and free.

*Discard every self-seeking
motive as soon as it is seen,
and you need not search for
truth; truth will find you.*

Sri Nisargadatta Maharaj.

RELATIVE & ABSOLUTE REALITY

Much does he gain, who when he loses, learns.
Michelangelo

No snowflake ever falls in the wrong place.

Zen

How can we fight the good fight in this crazy world without panicking about the possible outcome? By thoroughly understanding that, at the very same moment that I may be losing the fight of my life, *all is right with the Universe.* You can afford to go for broke and care intensely about making positive changes on this dear troubled planet, while still not sacrificing your basic sanity over it. We are immersed in the world, yet not submerged by it. Play your part well, though you know it's "only a play." Cosmically seen, all circumstances and scenarios happening are lawful.. and enlightening.

On the absolute level, everything is perfect. Yet at the same time, "relative reality" demands that you act, consciously, with passion and conviction, sometimes urgently. So, act from within enlightened intent; with big mind, for the good of All. Where necessary, resist and oppose what you know to be wrong - within you *and* outside - yet all the while and ultimately, not seduced by the duality of "us & them," "good & evil," the sooner to extricate us all from the suffering of separateness.

Be humble, for you are made of dung.
Be noble, for you are made of stars.

Serbian Proverb

A Great Hindu Lesson

In the beloved spiritual epic from India, the *Bhagavad Gita,* the troubled protagonist, Arjuna, faces a classic moral dilemma. Poised on a great battlefield between two massive armies, he is appalled at the prospect of having to lead a bloody fight against his own relatives. He implores God (In the form of Krishna, his charioteer) to advise him. Lord Krishna's answer is revered among the great timeless passages in world religious literature:

These temporal bodies are only said to die, but they are embodiments of the Eternal, which is indestructible and immeasurable. Therefore, great warrior, carry on thy fight.
The one who thinks he kills, and the one who believes he is killed, are both mistaken. IT neither kills nor is IT killed.
Unborn, the Self cannot die. Eternal, changeless, ancient, It does not perish with the body...
...And so, if you are a warrior, do not hesitate to fulfill your calling..
...Look with the same eyes upon pleasure and pain, loss and gain, victory and defeat... and you will not suffer evil.

***

BEGIN WHERE YOU ARE

*During the period of struggle, one should follow
the method of discrimination: "Not this, not this" -
and direct the whole mind to God.*

*But the state of Perfection is quite different.
After reaching God, one re-affirms what formerly one denied...
After realizing God, one knows definitely that it is He who has
become everything.*

Sri Ramakrishna.

*It is being human in the simplest and fullest sense.
That is the miracle and the adventure now.*

Richard Moss, M.D.

It has never been easy for individuals to extricate themselves from ignorance, fear, and greed. At the dawn of the twenty-first century, the obstacles to liberation are formidable indeed. And yet, ironically, the teachings of all truth-bearing enlightened paths and methods are now universally available for the first time in history. So omnipresent is the knowledge that you merely have to ask for it to appear. The opportunities are unprecedented (although so are the dangers).

*At the moment you are most in awe
of all there is about life that you don't understand,
you are closer to understanding than at any other time.*

Jane Wagner

It is no accident that you are reading this. The bell tolls for thee. It's time to go within and begin. Clean up your act. Purify yourself. Train your mind and body, and prepare for your test. Enlightenment is where you find it, and where you take it. Become your own hero.

Embarking on this, the ultimate quest, you may lose friends and gain critics. Fear not. You will be equal to the challenge if you keep love in your heart, and Enlightenment in your eyes. You are purified by your own pure intention.

WAYS OF TRANSFORMATION

*Now, in order that you may learn to know Me, so that
you can be **sure** it is I, your own True Self, Who speaks
these words, you must first learn to **Be Still,** to quiet
your human mind and body and all their activities, so
that you no longer are conscious of them.*

Joseph Benner's *The Impersonal Life*

Over the ages, those who have devoted their lives to such pursuits have developed reliable methods of awakening. Universal consciousness is best perceived when we are clear and poised. It helps to fertilize the ground for the germination of the sacred seeds of enlightenment. Even after spontaneous realization, we still need to anchor the experience in body and life, lest it fade into conceptual memory. Thus, we "sit" and meditate, or visualize, or pray or chant mantras, and do other non-usual *practices* that keep the mirror clean for the pure white light to reflect upon.

*We are caught in the prison of the mind. If we are to
escape, we must recognize that we are in prison.
If we think we are free, then no escape is possible.*

G.I. Gurdjieff

*We must besiege every cell of the brain, because that is
Where God is jailed.. seeking, trying, hammering to open
a gate in the fortress of matter.*

Nikos Kazantzakis

58

THE YOGA OF LIFE

Service without bondage is Yoga
Selfless work is Yoga
Balance of mind is Yoga
Ethical perfection is Yoga
Meditation is Yoga
Pure devotion is Yoga
***Enlightenment** is Yoga*
Cosmic Consciousness is Yoga
Come now, become a Yogi!

Yoga means "union," and the path to it: union of Self and Universe. It is Self-Knowledge, Self-Mastery, Self-Liberation. Self-Transcendence. Although we already have everything we require for happiness and understanding, a "path' is necessary because, we silly humans keep forgetting.

Choose a path with heart, and follow it as if your life depended on it. In the 21st century accelerated eclectic sectarian global culture, you will have to include everything you do, and everything that happens to you as part of your life-yoga: It's all living lessons and tests and spiritual soul food. Nothing is excluded on this path. Consecrate your passions. Place the image of your worst enemy on your spiritual alter. Breathe deeply 'till it feels good, even if it takes a lifetime.

Good Luck! On the steep path, obstacles and seduction appear just when you feel most resolved, like the aroma of a delicious hot meal when you're fasting. *THIS IS A TEST.* The most difficult thing in the world to master is oneself, yet it is the only thing worth doing. Become a warrior for Truth, and vanquish the false pretender to the throne: the puny superficial persona. Perform the alchemy of the soul and wake up to your own immortality. Child of Creation, it's time to realize your Godhead - without letting it go to your head.

*The True System of Yoga is to catch
the thread of one's own
consciousness.. and to hold on to it,
and go to the very end.*

Satprem

MEDITATION: THE SEAT OF ENLIGHTENMENT

*True spiritual practice springs <u>from,</u>
not <u>toward,</u> Enlightenment.*

Ken Wilber

*When we don't aspire, time creates us. But
when we aspire, we create time.*

Sri Chinmoy

*W*hy *is the crew of Spaceship Earth at war with itself at this late date? Why is
peace so elusive if I am in fact One with the Creator of the Universe? How come
I'm still confused and nervous?*

Though there's nowhere to go, we must step on the path and embark on our
quest. Since we don't know our true nature, we struggle, if only against the
illusion of our own mistaken identity. It is only because we are so habituated to
doing, that meditation - the quintessential act of only *being* - appears like
effort. In fact, meditation, by definition, is the cessation of all trying.

Slow Down The Action

*If there is no meditation, then you are like a blind man in
a world of great beauty, light and colour.*

Krishnamurti

Ordinarily, we perceive reality only approximately.. just as a motion picture is
actually merely light projected through transparent film and reflected on a
screen - a blurred succession of many flat, still images. You may become totally
involved in the illusion of action, and have a genuine, visceral response,
completely forgetting that it is all done with light and mirrors.

61

Similarly, the "real" world we live in and react to is a projection on the screen of our senses and filtered through the narrow mental lenses of predisposed desires, beliefs, expectations, opinions, fears, and needs.

Meditation cures the myopia of the personalized world view. To meditate is to slow down the movie; to more clearly perceive context over content; to recognize the compulsive distortions we impose on existence; to experience universal awareness.

This is not something "far-out." Meditation arises from and expresses your already-enlightened natural mind. *Meditating is choosing to embrace the radical truth of the suchness of the present and perfect omni-dimensional universal life within and without, here and now.*

*Space
is a function of time,
is a function of light,
is a function of Mind.*

Nadar

SIT, AND YE SHALL FIND

*Thoughts and concepts are all that block us
from always being, quite simply, in the absolute.*
Sogyal Rinpoche

The very source of creativity is enlightened mind. Whether you are a hard-working gardener, middle-level office manager, stressed-out parent, beleaguered spouse, amateur musician, fitness instructor, prison inmate, construction worker, a sanitation engineer or frustrated novelist, a hair dresser, freelance entrepreneur, homeless person, soldier or senator, meditation can help. Suddenly or slowly, soon or eventually, you come into your true potential, and excel at what you do without having to buy an instruction book, go anywhere, or believe anything taught by anyone. You merely have to *sit*.

*Natural Enlightenment exists prior to any spiritual
practice. Paths are illusory.*
Lex Hixon

*The real voyage of discovery consists not in seeking
new landscapes, but in having new eyes.*

Marcel Proust

Lonny J. Brown

Good for Humans

Meditation is like chicken soup: It's *good* for you. A unique brain activity distinct from both active thinking and unconscious sleep, meditation turns out to be healthy as well as enlightening. It is the quintessential antidote for the stresses of modern civilization, and simultaneously the best way to prepare for your inevitable departure from this fleeting life.

Not incidentally, meditation is preventive and remedial for a wide range of physical disorders, including those of the muscles, nerves, and the circulatory, digestive, hormonal and respiratory systems. With practice, it can reduce high blood pressure and eliminate migraine headaches, asthma attacks, and spastic colitis. The body's immune system is also strengthened by meditation.

Neurological tests reveal that the brain receives 60% more oxygen when subjects commence meditating, significantly improving clarity of mind, receptivity and learning capacities. A harmonization occurs between the cerebral cortex - the conscious, socialized part of the brain - and the diencephalon, the instinctual, subconscious part. We are no longer fighting ourselves internally. The autonomic nervous system allows a relaxation response, consisting of a drop in muscle tension, lower heart rate and blood pressure, slower breathing. This entire response is the exact opposite of the body's reaction to stress. During meditation, all the organs rest and conserve energy. There are immediate benefits to one's overall wellness.

On the mental/emotional front, meditation tends to moderate anxiety and depression, often as an adjunct to biofeedback and counseling. Typical results include reduced defensiveness and aggression, greater sense of peace, self-esteem and confidence, better communication, and more patience, optimism, and humor. Because it bilaterally integrates the right (artistic) and left (rational) brain hemispheres, meditation can significantly enhance the higher faculties of memory, intuition, and creativity.

Spiritually, meditation is often a catalyst for greater insight into one's purpose and role in life, a sense of unity and connectedness, and an understanding of the meaning of one's challenges. Often it becomes the doorway to a source of inner strength and guidance, particularly to people facing extreme stress and life-threatening illness.

64

What Meditation Is:
Quieting and clearing the mind.. Attending inward.. Opening perception.. A way of centering and balance.. Coming into the present.. A source of inspiration and guidance.. A psycho-super-natural healing.. A tool for self-inquiry and discovery.. Working on oneself.. Intrinsic freedom.. Conscious living.. Deepening and expanding awareness..

Meditation is awareness, not thought. It is occupying your original essence of awareness.

Meditation is the optimal strategy for moving into *authentic livingness*. It is a simple but profound human activity; the best opportunity to vacate the identity which you are usually compelled to project in daily life, and assume your basic enlightened nature. It offers insight into non-duality, and relieves you of the heavy burden of having to fight or fear the world.

Meditation is sublime and mundane, sometimes effortless, sometimes difficult. Like climbing a mountain, it is its own reward, *on the path or at the summit*. The more you engage in it, the more self-evident and profound it becomes.

Be True To Your School

Meditation comes in a variety of shapes and styles, and – particularly for westerners - choosing is rather like shopping for a new car: You may need to sit in a few and drive them around to discern which suits you best. Then you make your choice, take it home, and use it, hopefully for years of reliable transportation.. or *transformation*.

There are focused meditations, with "objects" both internal and external, such as a candle flame, or one's breath, a mantra, or the psychic energy centers (*chakras*), along the spine. You can meditatively contemplate metaphysical concepts, levels of reality, or positive qualities of being, such as compassion. There are devotional contemplations on deity, guided visualizations, and healing meditations. There is also "empty," objectless meditation, which develops faculties of mindfulness, bare attention, and insight. In all, meditation is the opposite of distraction, daydreaming, mental dispersion and unconsciousness. The center of all meditative approaches is the same: the ultimate freedom of Enlightenment.

Just Do It.

> *At the five sense doors*
> *spread the net of mindfulness so fine and subtle.*
> *In it defilements will be caught,*
> *and can be extinguished by insight clear.*

> - Anuruddha Thera

Spontaneous realization is the culmination of lifetimes of good, hard work. As potentially profound as its effects may be, the act of meditation is nothing dramatic or special at all. In fact, it can often seem quite boring. Yet the ceaseless demand for activity is precisely the type of mental addiction that prevents us from seeing our true nature and the very quality and depth of life.

Slowly replacing the incessant striving of surface thinking, meditation has a way of insinuating a certain deeper peace into our busy existence that is available through almost no other way. Still, the beginner must be eminently patient with the restless brain.

Keeping Still

The most conducive environment for meditation is clean, warm, quiet, and free of distractions. Make it special, keep it simple: soft lighting, a few images of inspiring role models, symbols of perfection, or objects of natural beauty, such as a flower or crystal. The meditation space becomes a symbolic sanctuary and actual gateway through which you realize your truest nature, the purity of your being.

Becoming Meditatively Mindful

> *Thoughts are birds,*
> *Feelings are clouds*
> *Emotions are rain*
> *Breath is the wind*
> *I am the sky*

> Elam

66

OK, there you are in your favorite quiet spot, seated, balanced, relaxed, with no urgent obligations, and nothing to distract you.. except of course the incessant running commentary of your own neurotic mind: *" Did I forgot to turn off the phone? I wonder what time it is. What was that noise? It's probably the cat.. Lucky animal has nothing to worry about. My back hurts.. I wonder when I'll get enlightened.. I think I'll have scrambled eggs for breakfast.. It sure would be great having sex with... "*

Is this meditation? Hardly. To be worth the time, meditation must be different than just plain old daydreaming. *We do not meditate in English.* Yet, as inane and irrelevant as your habitual wayward thoughts may be, it is utterly futile to resist them. Such battling only generates more mental commotion and frustration.

(Pay attention now.. here comes the heart and soul of this instruction. Get this, and you're well on your way..)

A compassionate, patient approach to quelling the compulsive thinking process without fighting it entails <u>giving thoughts room to come and go, witnessed by non-judging awareness.</u> Practice acknowledging and releasing thoughts, instead of fighting or following them. "Label" your activity *thinking, thinking,* and know yourself as the sentience behind the sense. Again and again, sooner and sooner, gently bring your attention back to your meditative center of focus (be it the belly, the breath, an image, a mantra, or ultimately, pure objectless awareness itself), in the here and now of being. Remember:

I am not my thoughts; I am the living, breathing Spirit of the Universe, in the Eternal Now who thinks, feels, cares can cries, yet abides untouched.

The undisciplined mind is like a child at a huge carnival. It is naturally curious and tantalized by the sights and sounds around it. The challenge is to interest the child-mind in the single chosen object before you. To reprimand or hold on too tightly would only create conflict and aversion. Instead, persistently offer the alternative to arbitrary distractions and seductions. Eventually the deeper, more focused meditative awareness becomes increasingly dominant, and attention is naturally inclined to stay still for longer periods.

Thoughts are like birds in the vast blue sky of your greater awareness. Notice objectively and dispassionately the arising ideas, images, memories, feelings, impulses.. and then just let them fly by. Eventually, this very *letting go* happens sooner and sooner, until awareness remains "unruffled" by anything, for longer and longer periods of time. Thus the witness no longer identifies with the thoughts.

Treat thoughts, images, memories, feelings, and all mental events just as you do successive breaths, with <u>choiceless awareness</u>, without judgment or reaction: allow them to arise, exist, and disperse through the vastness of the witnessing mind, without clinging or following. Notice the space between. Return ever sooner to the present center of your being, and you will find that "distractions" become merely energy events to expanded awareness. This is mindfulness, the basis of conscious living, a powerful beacon of pure awareness shining over the perilous sea of life.

> Without grasping, leave the hearing in the hearing, leave the seeing in the seeing, without letting your attachment enter into the perception.
>
> Sogyal Rinpoche.

Mindfulness is the mirror of self-remembering. The witness. Awareness without preference, the non-judging, non-reacting Knower. Dispassionate, impartial, mindfulness is the view that enlightens you to suchness: *that which is*, when the vehicle, the path and the goal are one; when the knower knows its Self.

> At some point when the mind is silenced and our real self can be felt inwardly, we will feel the ecstasy of the free flow of spiritual energy throughout our being. We will feel bliss, inner light, release from time and space, freedom from individuality and its fear, conflict and suffering. We will experience that great Divine Power which is in the center of our being and we will now know that God is within us.
>
> Joseph Benner (The Impersonal Life)

ENLIGHTENMENT IN YOUR BODY

There's no use reaching for the stars if you're not comfortable in your skin.

Nadar

Many spiritual seekers think enlightenment is a metaphysical achievement; that is, beyond the physical. They assume that "deliverance" involves *transcendence* of the material world of form, including the body. Religious asceticism and the renunciation of sex result from this displaced view, as does the concept of "heaven" as reachable only when we drop our bodies.

This historic but dysfunctional schism between consciousness and matter, spirit and flesh, leads to all kinds of problems, including disassociation, alienation and guilt. It gave rise to the centuries-old turf battle between science and religion, and it perpetually postpones the very realization we seek.

The Truth of Life can never be found *out there.* First and foremost, it's right *here*, in your gut, your heart, your breath, your bowels. You *are* the Living Spirit of the Universe, but you'll never realize it if you can't relax in your own body.

Meditation is often used as a subtle form of escape: people sit still in order to *get out.* Astral projection feels like "liberation." But, in the practical parlance of the chakra system, the lotus crown is connected to the muddy root - the very source of our energy - itself originating in the dark, dirty earth. As the Buddha so poignantly taught, life hurts, but the solution is not avoidance (which is impossible), but complete openness to life.

The first lessons in meditation literally begin with your seat, and deal with physical mechanics like balance, alignment, and relaxation. After these come sensory, breath and energy awareness, and perceiving our own mind at work. It is through investigating the very real-world, human condition that accurate insight arises. We finally see the miraculous in just what is, which is, in reality, all there ever was or will be.

69

MEDITATION FOR PEOPLE WITH BODIES

*Within the body there is played music unending, though
without stringed instruments. That music of the Word pervades
the entire creation. Who listens to it is freed from all illusion,
And through it meets the True Lord face to face.*

Kabir

To still the mind, begin by easing the body. Liberation is first of all a physical experience: the sense of balance, free breathing, and deep relaxation are bodily gates to the psycho-spiritual dimension of undisturbed awareness. In meditation, as in all healing and transformation, nothing really happens if it doesn't happen all through you. If it's real, *you know it in your gut.*

The physical preliminaries for meditation consist of creating uprightness, balance, and release. Vertically align your spine. You needn't have your legs tied in knots like a Himalayan ascetic. Sitting cross-legged on a cushion or straight up on a chair will suffice, so long as the spine is erect.

That's upright, not uptight. Most of the muscles in the body should be relaxed by the time you settle in for meditation. Unfortunately, this may be easier said than done.

How to Relax
One of the most effective tension-relieving techniques takes the paradoxical approach of systematically tightening the body before relaxing it. It is called *progressive relaxation* because the muscles are flexed and released individually, in sequence. The tightening should be done upwards - from the feet to the head (one area or muscle group at a time) - and the loosening in reverse order, from the top down (with the pull of gravity).

For best results, inhale strongly through the nostrils while increasing the tension, and exhale suddenly through the mouth when releasing it. Repeat this cycle for each limb and muscle throughout the body. Follow with systematic sequential relaxation: attentively and deliberately relinquishing all traces of holding, from head to toes, giving over your body weight to the earth, until you feel thoroughly passive and loose all over. This method engenders an uncanny feeling of freedom and lightness, of floating *within* the body.

How To Breathe

All things in nature breathe, but only humans manage to get it wrong. To breathe effortlessly is to remember your true nature, which is to taste Enlightenment. This can easily take a lifetime to happen, or occur this very moment.

"The way of the breath ("Pranayama") brings us in touch with a profound part of our nature. At the meeting place between voluntary and involuntary action, the breath (or more accurately, the force that breathes you) is none other than the spiritual energy of Life Itself. Discovering this - experiencing it completely in your body - enriches one immediately and infinitely. Awareness through breath is supreme among methods: simple, profound, powerful.

Self-Healing and Consciousness Expansion through Passive Breath Awareness

A profound personal health and development practice known to yogi's and meditators for millennia is as available as your own breath. This simple technique, called *Passive Breath Awareness*, deeply relaxes the body, calms the nervous system, and fosters spiritual insight. It is an ideal stress buster, promoting inner peace and renewing one's energy. You only have to try this method for a few minutes to experience positive improvements in your body and mind.

Breathing is usually automatic and thoughtless. Evolution has insured that our breathing dynamically mirrors the moment-to-moment dynamics of life as we navigate and cope with our material (and emotional) existence. Fast or labored breathing indicates exertion or stress, while regular, slow breathing accompanies relaxation, recovery, sleep, and regeneration. What many people don't realize is that we can access and improve various physical, mental and emotional functions through working with the breath. In other words, conscious, deliberate, slow deep breathing is good for you! (It feels great too.)

Bridging the mind/body interface, breathing holds the unique property of being either voluntary or automatic. It goes on indefinitely without our conscious consideration, but - unlike your heartbeat and other functions - you can "hold" or slow down the breath at will - thereby breaking the unconscious feedback loop between the sympathetic and parasympathetic functions of the autonomic nervous system. The potentials for this type of conscious breath auto-regulation are great. It can help improve serious medical conditions such as hypertension, asthma, migraines, and more. It is also the gateway to inner spiritual consciousness.

The meditative breath is the opposite of controlled breathing. It starts with regular, two-part diaphragmatic breathing. [illustration A]. The first part, the inhalation, naturally involves some initial active force. The physical mechanism of the in-breath primarily entails the distension of the belly, more than the expansion of the rib cage. (You can verify this with your hand over your belly: it swells out upon inhalation.)

Part two of the breath cycle is exhalation, and the beginning of the effortless release stage of Passive Breath Awareness (PBA). Just as you can voluntarily relax and "drop" your outer limbs or abdominal muscles, you can relax the large horizontal flat diaphragm muscle within your belly. Feel this release while letting out a full breath: the extended diaphragm contracts and flattens the tummy, emptying the lungs.

A relaxation breath begins with a deep inhalation, followed by a deep release, and subsequent smaller and slower breaths (illustrations B & C).

We usually think of breathing as two-part (in and out), but there is a third distinct component of the breath cycle, and it comes between the other two. [illustration D] At the "bottom" of each exhalation, before it turns into inhalation, there is a moment of *motionlessness*, called the still-point. Through deeper relaxation after each exhalation, the still-point increases in duration (illustration E). This is the gateway to the remarkable realm of Passive Breath Awareness.

An excellent method of training in three-part breath awareness is to coordinate it with a three-part mental mantra, such as Be Here Now (with the *now* corresponding to the still-point).

Breath Yoga
(practice on an empty stomach)

Phase one: CONTROLLED BREATHING.

Cleansing Breath.
> In sequence, force all air from the belly, rib cage, and shoulders, out through the mouth. Cough if necessary.
Charging Breath.
> Breathe in deeply through the nostrils, strongly pulling the air in and down, to expand the belly, then the chest, lifting the rib cage and finally the shoulders.
> Repeat the cycle 3 times, with increasingly deep breaths.
> Hold the breath in while tightening the body.
> Release the breath and the body simultaneously.
> Repeat Controlled Breathing, but end by releasing the body before the breath.

Phase two: PASSIVE BREATH AWARENESS

> Continue belly breathing, but passively, without effort. Seat your awareness in the originating center of the breath. Attention rides the surface of the diaphragm like a feather barely floating on the surface of a still pond.
> Expand full passive breath awareness upwards over the full length and volume of the lungs.
> Change to awareness of inbreath, outbreath, and the stillpoint between them (at the "bottom" of each exhalation).
> Relax your whole body completely with each exhalation, naturally allowing the stillpoint *and your relaxation* to extend in duration.
> Bring the attention ever deeper inward.
> Experience the whole breath-body co-terminal with and permeating the physical.
> Meditatively investigate the energy of the belly center (*hara* / 3rd chakra), thoroughly, repeatedly.
> Mentally send breath-energy surging to all areas of the body.
> An excellent method of training in three-part breath awareness is to coordinated it with a three-part mental mantra, such as Be Here Now, with now corresponding to the stillpoint.
Consciously heal self and others with projected breath-body awareness.

With the breath flowing thoroughly free, meditatively ask the question: *Who or What is breathing me?*

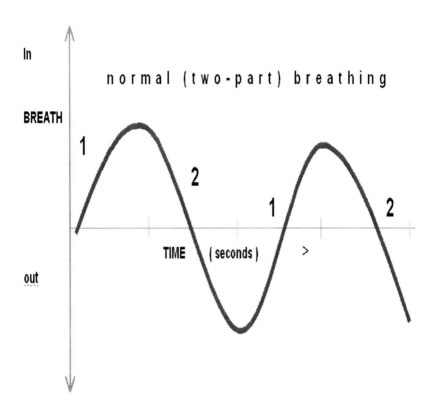

A.

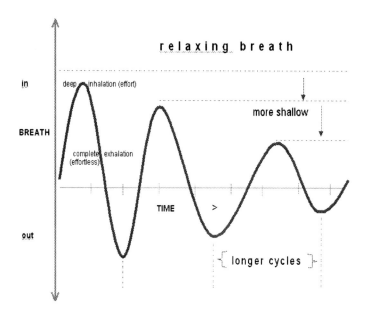

relaxing breath

◇ Taking a **relaxing breath** entails shifting from controlled to automatic (*passive*) breathing. An initial deep inhalation and complete exhalation are followed by progressively more shallow and slower breathing, with the emphasis on letting go.

B.

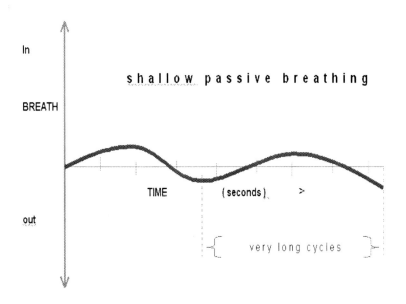

❖ Breathing is shallow and slow during sleep, meditation, or in the case of many animals, during hibernation. The body is deeply relaxed, and even though overall oxygen consumption decreases, a greater percentage goes to the central nervous system, accompanied by quieter brain wave patterns. Practicing passive breath awareness (PBA) comfortably induces this uniquely beneficial and enjoyable metabolic state.

C.

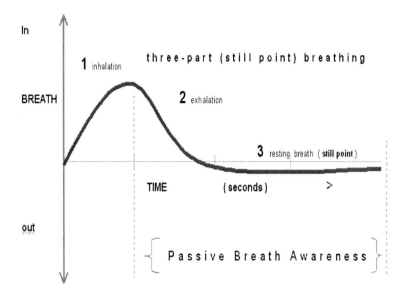

⟡ The practice of **passive breath awareness** utilizes a third breath component, called the **stillpoint**, after the exhalation, before inhalation resumes. At this juncture - with the body sufficiently at rest and oxygen requirements minimal - breathing is so rested that it momentarily ceases. The duration of this motionless phase of the breath cycle gradually increases with practice.

D.

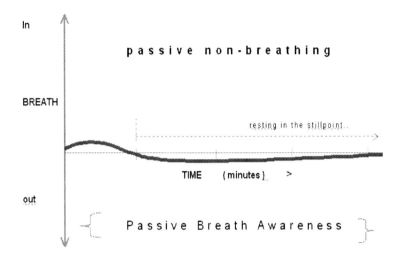

In

BREATH

out

passive non-breathing

resting in the stillpoint..

TIME (minutes) >

Passive Breath Awareness

◇ **Passive Breath Awareness** physiologically leads to extremely slow and shallow breathing with extended breath-less pauses. Unexpectedly, such non-breathing is completely comfortable, sometimes even euphoric. The practice extends the passive "effortlessness" of the out-breath to the next inhalation as well.

E.

A light, white feather barely touches the surface of a still pool
of clear water at the bottom of a deep, silent well.

My awareness is the feather.
The smooth, lightly undulating surface
is the free-floating diaphragm bridging my belly cavity.
The crystal clear pool is the deeper consciousness within.
OM.

I am free within the breath, the body, the world, the Universe.

<u>Body Enlightenment Meditation</u>

Arriving, on the spot, quiet, my pure intention is enlightening.
My spine lifts vertically, honorably,
from the earth's core to the sky and beyond.
I fill up with fresh air, then settle down around each out-breath,
becoming completely balanced (side-to-side, front-to-back, top-to-bottom

To the great gravitational pull of the planet I release my limbs,
relaxing all muscles (top-down, outside-in, large-to-small, head-to-toes)
This semi-solid organism settles into poised stillness.

Sensing breathing.. floating all around this fully automatic natural
movement;
dropping ever deeper through each exhalation,
and into the motionless, open stillness underneath,
verifying that indeed, life breathes me.
This is extremely relaxing.

The living planet's own energy emanates into me from below,
up the electrified spine, opening all glands and organs,
releasing and circulating their fluids.
Rushing through my heart,
echoing silence,
light and color illuminate this brain and consciousness.

Beholding the Inner Light,
I am sentience-in-matter,
none other than the Creator recreating the creation,
on the spot.

ljb

PROFOUND RELAXATION

*The atoms and molecules within you
dream they are people.*
Seth

Core relaxation is the art of throwing one's metabolism into neutral and coasting on its miraculous natural, perpetual momentum. The experience is one of floating within the space of your own physical form - free of its confinement and weight, yet infused with its pulsating energy. The entire organism is on auto-pilot. Small interior muscles relax as well as the larger limbs, felt down to the cellular level. Core relaxation includes postural alignment and balance, neuro-motor quieting, passive breathing, and open energy flow. This is the deepest level of *super-conscious relaxation.*

Going Deeper

Everyone who's ever taken a hot bath knows the wonderful feeling of thoroughly relaxing the body. But this physical level is just the beginning of the deeper, all encompassing relaxation process. Really complete ("profound") relaxation includes the muscles, nerves, organs, glands, circulation, energy, brain and mind, and effects one's whole being.

Imagine you are on retreat at a beautiful secluded health spa. You've just returned from a refreshing walk in the woods, feeling comfortably "spent." After enjoying some delicious herbal tea by the fireplace, you retire to shower, then bathe in a soothing hot tub, complete with pulsing water jets stimulating your skin and relaxing your muscles. You then enter a warm, softly lit healing room, complete with beautiful candles, flower-essence aromas, calming music and an inviting massage table and practitioner.

Here, at the healing hands of an exceptionally skillful master massage therapist, all remaining traces of aches and tension are totally drawn from your grateful body. With loose limbs, energy flowing, and skin glowing, you thoroughly appreciate this most completely relaxing experience in your life.. and you vow to remember it.

If the bad news is you can hardly afford this kind of extraordinary treatment any time soon, the good news is that *you can voluntarily return to that state of deep relaxation - and more - at will, at home, on a regular basis.* The mastery of such a practice is the virtual enlightenment of the body.

Happily, the way to this most profound form of relaxation is becoming widely available just when civilization needs it more than ever. An increasing number of people involved with yoga, meditation, contemplative prayer, biofeedback, hypnosis, and other intentional inner-directed self-development practices are discovering the mental/emotion/spiritual dimensions of relaxation. These holistic auto-regulatory, self-healing methods naturally calm the body, quiet the mind, and balance internal energies.

Recognizing that we have physical, mental, emotional, subconscious and spiritual aspects of our being, the holistic approach to auto-regulation and deep relaxation is multi-dimensional, organic, and progressive. In other words, we use a variety of mind/body techniques that create deeper and more reliable results over time. Obviously, this requires an investment of effort somewhat greater than simply popping a pill, but even just a few minutes a day can yield rewards, and they only get better with regular practice; with practice you can learn to relax deeper, faster and easier.

This Relaxation Response beneficially affects all stress variables, including muscle tension, blood pressure, stress-hormone production, breathing, etc. It is the physiological component of meditation. It not only feels wonderful, but a growing body of clinical evidence shows it to be therapeutic, preventive, performance-enhancing, and life-extending.[2]

As mentioned, profound relaxation includes the muscles and limbs, but also goes to the very deepest levels of our being. In addition to the extremities letting go, blood vessels dilate, circulation and energy are optimized, the breath is freed, the senses quieted, the brain and central nervous system balance, and the mind is stilled. This is literally relaxation to the core, achieved through a series of concentric withdrawals of all effort, holding, or distraction.

Medically, practicing profound relaxation can significantly improve high blood pressure, headaches, asthma, immune problems, back ache, insomnia and digestive disorders. On mental / emotional / psychological levels, the regular practice of deep relaxation can help in overcoming anxiety and phobias, focusing attention and enhancing concentration, correcting certain behavioral disorders, and improving self-esteem.

82

Metabolically, core relaxation goes beyond even the sleep-state. Because it is done intentionally and consciously, brain and body are quieted simultaneously, and the mind gets to enjoy the results. It is free-floating in time and space, with a deep, abiding sense of peace. In energy anatomy, this occurs when the internal centers (charkas), are all simultaneously "open."

Spiritually, deep relaxation helps us move beyond body and ego identity to more transcendent experiences of wholeness, unity, and the timeless and infinite dimensions of existence. It is from this state of super-relaxation that peace, joy, cosmic insights and spiritual enlightenment are fostered.

True relaxation is an opportunity to experience ourselves as human beings, as opposed to human *doings*. Action is replaced with pure knowing. Although the breath flows, the heart beats, and the body automatically performs a million subtle functions, the experience is one of total non-effort. Consciousness is withdrawn from the external senses[3] but remains fully aware. One's center of knowing effortlessly resides within free-floating internal space, in absolute stillness. This inner absorption is called samadhi in Zen, and the ancient Yoga Sutras of Patanjali describe it as the *ceasing of the oscillations of the mind*, which is true Self-realization.

As impressive as this sounds, this deep level of relaxation is available to nearly everyone. You don't have to study esoteric cosmologies or take a spiritual retreat or to experience it. It merely requires training and practice. *You can get there from here.*

---

[3] *pratyahara* in yoga, systematic sense withdrawal

Meditation, Centering and Balance

The heart of meditation is consistent practice. Ironically, the greatest obstacle is one's own inertia. We need to meditate regularly, often, over many seasons, to gain the full potential of this precious method. It's that simple, and that difficult.

Please Sit

> *Meditatively focus on your subtle sense of balance within the three spatial dimensions: front-to-back, side-to-side, and top-to-bottom.*

> *Delicately locate and fix your awareness in your center of gravity, within the belly-center, allowing it to relax ever deeper, with each exhalation. Reside only here, over and over. Being in fullness.. effortless.. there is no holding, no going forth. No boundary, no direction, only the immediacy of the energy within. Here is the very beginning and center of the Enlightened body.*

> *Look!*
> *There's absolutely no difference*
> *between common and cosmic.*
> *All is miraculous!*

- Nadar

84

TEACHERS ARE MIRRORS

Your own self is your ultimate teacher.
The outer teacher is merely a milestone.
It is only your inner teacher that will walk
with you to the goal, for he is the goal.

Sri Nisargadatta Maharaj

There comes a time on the quest when it helps to have a good teacher - a "spiritual friend" - who can accurately monitor your progress (or lack thereof), and tell you what you need to hear when you are ready to hear it.

Such a mentor will appear when you are ready (although it may be when you least expect it). He or she may be a recognized master, or an anonymous stranger; male or female, young or old, modest or outrageous, depending on what you need, but if you are totally dedicated to acquiring wisdom, rest assured the teacher will appear. Great teachers may still be rare, but today they have great reach, and they **love** enlightening people! The Sufis say *Take one step towards Allah and he takes ten steps towards you.*

It will be up to you to determine your prospective teacher's authenticity and integrity, for there are many false pretenders waiting to capitalize on people's ignorance and spiritual hunger. In the spiritual supermarket as elsewhere, discriminating awareness is required. If you give away your good judgment to a cosmic con artist, you will surely get burned. Of course that too will be a valuable teaching.

The relationship between a realized teacher and the devoted student is a most sacred and magical one. It is based on absolute trust, love and devotion. Within this super-natural bond, telepathy becomes possible, personal evolution is accelerated, and transformation blossoms. The master/disciple relationship is the ultimate spiritual proving ground.

Where the Spirit is, there is freedom.
And we, with our unveiled faces
reflecting like mirrors the brightness of
the Lord, all grow brighter and
brighter as we are turned into the
image that we reflect.
St. Paul

Even without a physical guide, the Universe in its infinite wisdom has a way of continually providing teachings, for those who seek. No doubt you can go a long way - lifetimes - without gurus, provided you listen, and take to heart what is revealed. The best teacher shows you exactly when and how you do *not* need a teacher, for you and the guru and God are in truth One. Eventually, every student must teach.

HAVE YOU MET HER?

We are all lying in the gutter,
but some of us are looking at the stars

Oscar Wilde.

*H*er honesty is so obvious and absolute that you trust her completely. Her countenance is simply beautiful. Her clear eyes penetrate you own with intensity and integrity, and she effortlessly reads your secret thoughts. There is nowhere to hide from her Universal Love.

She speaks with her eyes and her smile and her whole body and soul, and much is conveyed in the silence. In an audience of a thousand, you could swear she is addressing you alone, her words resonating to the very core of your being. She answers all your questions, eases your mind, and frees your heart. And she challenges you to become your best possible expression of the same divine love and wisdom.

Upon meeting such a rare being, it is altogether appropriate to offer your utmost respect, not for her sake, but for your own purification, and for the benefit of a needful world. These are the precious lights among us that keep the world from going dark. Their very presence offers hope, dispels confusion and redeems our predicament. If you are ready - clear and clean, without arrogance or self-pity - it is worth waiting (and working) a lifetime to meet such an enlightened soul, for the effect is gloriously contagious.

Have you already met her, and missed the chance to see? Don't worry.. your yearning and your readiness will bring her back again.

THE GURU AND YOU

Spiritual guidance is the art of making a being become what he or she is. The pupil senses beyond his personality that divine model which he is, yet of which he is only vaguely aware. The teacher is supposed to make him see what he is rather than tell him what he should be.

Pir Vilayat -Khan

It is a very special day, though you may not yet realize how special. Perhaps you sense a momentous change approaching..

You have been waiting for this day for a long, long time. A life time? Longer. Destiny has arranged the most important rendezvous of your life for today: the meeting with your beloved Guru.

Each of us, whether we know it or not, is being watched and guided by a higher intelligence who takes great interest in our soul's evolution. This being - you may call them your super-natural friend, your Guiding Angel, Holy Saint or Great Grandfather - knows you infinitely better than you know yourself. He (or She) knows your essence and your facade, the games you play, the sins you've committed, the pain you've suffered. The Guru loves you more than you could possibly imagine. He/she knows what you want, as a personality, and what you *need*, as a soul-student in the school of life. The Master knows the odds against your recognizing the difference.

Are you psychologically equipped to meet your own Guru? Would you even recognize him or her? Would your habitual mind prevent you from understanding this being or learning from them? If so, a tremendous conflict would arise from such a premature revelation.

Out of the greatest compassion and respect, your spiritual mentor has refrained from interfering with your life. Over a thousand incarnations, he watched from a distance, as you learned the hard way, by trail and error, about natural spiritual law. Though your pain was his pain, like an anxious but wise and patient parent, he never violated your freedom to learn from your own mistakes. Sometimes he would assume a disguise and come into your life to drop a hint, or give some encouragement or solace. Sometimes he would help heal you while you slept. But never would he impose his will on yours, or force your awakening.

In this way the truths you so painstakingly arrived at could be wholly embraced as your own. Your sense of morality and justice was hard-earned by all the karma of your mistakes and offences. Your quest for the answers about life and death, creation, the universe, and your own purpose became a genuine, deep-seated yearning, tempered by the burning up of all other desires and distractions. Finally you could look up, beyond your personal concerns, with a sense of humility and awe. You could ask for understanding; you could properly pray for guidance.

You have no idea how joyous this moment is for your unseen ally. Think of all the time he waited, with infinite forbearance, with more faith in you than you had in yourself, while you took your two steps forward, one back...

Today's step will finally bring you face to face.

With his transcendent knowledge of karma and timing, the holy one had arranged your first conscious meeting as Master and disciple. You remember it well. No language can adequately convey the importance of such a momentous rendezvous; the overwhelming power of recognition, like finally coming home, to total forgiveness; the complete infusion of Divine Love. It was a first fresh deep breath after eons of suffocation.

In your mind you try to slow down and review that fateful event to extract and savor every moment. But it happened so swiftly. Before you knew it, it was over and done, and you were left standing there with your tears of joy, but also a fleeting frustration, at having been *taken* so unaware. Did you make the most of the opportunity? Could you have been more open? More attentive.. more grateful?

For a while you brood over these questions. How many people ever get to be in the presence of a Saint? And there you are, wishing for a second shot! You pray to be pure enough, worthy of receiving the blessing of just one more audience with the One who to you is the embodiment of Enlightened Mind.

By His grace your prayers have been answered. You will meet the Great Teacher again.

As you rise to meet this day, you begin a deliberate, almost ritualistic process of preparation. At an open window you salute the sun. In the shower, you take great care to wash thoroughly, in a holy purification rite, like a baptism.

Next you devote an hour to yoga and meditation, arriving at a deep inner calm which you will take into your day and journey. Finally you dress in new clothes, and venture out to begin your pilgrimage to His esteemed presence.

It will take many hours of travel, through city and country and city again. Though you take no food today, you move through the marketplace undistracted. All your senses are becoming sharper; your mind is one-pointed. His Name is your mantra. You will be ready.

As you walk, your steps are smooth and light. While driving, you are conscious of a perfect harmony among man, machine, and road. You pass the time chanting, blessing the birds and the billboards and the gas station attendants. How different the world becomes when you know you are on your way to be with a realized being. With each passing mile you become more open, more receptive. Intuitively you know that *this* time the transmission will be complete, and sufficient for a lifetime.

You finally arrive at the designated meeting house for your reunion with your Guru. Removing your shoes, you are shown to a waiting room, and visit a washroom to cleanse yourself. You take a long look in the mirror and make sure you are fully awake. You chuckle: it is like going to meet your maker. You take a deep breath and prepare to offer yourself totally and without reservation.

After a brief wait, you are ushered in to the inner hall. Immediately upon entering, you behold His seated form before you, and your gaze never strays to any other person in the room. That ancient feeling rushes over you like a tidal wave and your heart pounds hard within. But he is holding your eyes with his and you are uncannily calm and centered in the midst of all the power, witnessing the whole scenario in great equanimity. You do not feel like an agent of your actions. You find yourself bowing spontaneously, not in subservience, but out of deepest reverence. It is a surrender and a sharing.

The Great Teacher smiles. It is just a light smile, but his powerful love floods over you and melts your heart completely. He motions silently for you to sit on a cushion directly before him. You divert your eyes momentarily to complete the movement, and a thousand thoughts flood your joyous racing mind. Looking up, you come again under the radiance of his deep compassionate gaze, and you realize he knows every one of those thousand thoughts. You are naked and transparent. It is thrilling and exhilarating, and you know you could easily collapse at his feet, there to cry like a baby... but you do not move. He is taking you silently beyond emotion, to a state of perfect grace.

Here you rest, suspended in a seemingly breathless balance between past and future, coming and going, spirit and matter. There is nothing left to do, nowhere in this Universe you'd rather be. If you had any lingering doubts or questions, they have been answered and dissolved in the silent spaciousness of this transcendent shared awareness. You feel as if life's mystery has been revealed. You no longer cling to anything. Every in-breath is renewal, every out-breath is completion. And it is all God's good grace.

After an eternity in a moment, you realize he is going to say something, and you feel vaguely curious as to whether you might still be able to understand spoken language, for the intellect has long since been transcended. But his words are of course perfectly delivered to your heart and mind, and they come across simple and crystal clear: "You and I are One."

It is like a delayed-reaction nuclear depth-charge. Initially, for one long moment, it just settles in, past the first layers of the myopic, slightly cool cerebral cortex, which, like some kind of computer, automatically analyzes the words and efficiently stores them for further reflection. But suddenly, as your Master's eyes seem to intensify, the full realization explodes deep within your center. Into a swirling multicolored vortex of pure energy you fall, as the bottom simply drops away, and the sides too of your known world disperse into infinite space in all directions. All is.. Consummate Truth.. total revelation. Wow. You got it. You Are It. It is All. Glorious
Ah..

Useful Qualities to Cultivate

Moderation
Equanimity
Compassion
Reverence
Respect
Gratitude
Simplicity
Modesty
Patience
Perseverance
Faith
Joy
Love

HAVE YOU MET YOUR SELF?

What lies behind us, and what lies before us,
are tiny matters compared to what lies within us.

Emerson

*E*nlightened, the Universe is your home and you turn inside-out with the world. Generosity gets the best of you. You are crazy-wise. Your activity is spontaneous, un-prescribed, yet perfectly appropriate. You contain invisible power, but you are as modest as moisture. You know what needs to be done, and it gets done effortlessly, with grace and efficiency.

You can be invisible or fill the room. You are cool under stress, joyous whenever possible. Your timing is impeccable. Your touch heals, you can kill with a glance, but you leave 'em laughing when you go.

When you are in the flow of the Tao (the Way of Life), the future is now; all work is play, and pain is empty, making life an artistic pursuit rather than a struggle to survive and win. Enlightenment bestows the realization of the illusion of self, quitting all pretense of personal importance.. You are at once annihilated and liberated, although it looks as if nothing is happening.

SOLITUDE & SILENCE

*There is nothing in all the Universe
so much like God as silence*

Meister Eckhart

The way to freeing an over-worked brain of distractions and delusion begins with some kind of withdrawal from the horizontal, exterior world and one's everyday active role in it: a retreat environment where peace and quiet prevail, where you can take off your watch, be unavailable for phone calls, and become clear and calm for some extended period of time. Everyone deserves such a respite from their busy lives. We need to clear the air to see the light.

Don't just do something, sit there.

Thich Nhat Hanh

*Every life is fleeting.
Every day is Thanksgiving.*

Elam

94

MANTRA: TARGET PRACTICE

Mantra is a trick to bring the mind into awareness of one good thing instead of a million useless ones. It is a sacred phrase repeated mentally, continuously, with every breath you take, for as long as you can, until concentration is perfected, and the essence of its meaning is penetrated. Mantra accesses the same higher faculties as prayer, but it is not petitionary. It is scientific in the sense that it is a reliable tool, and spiritual in its intent and effect.

Mantra can become your super-natural reminder of your fully awakened awareness of your own true nature. It relies on repetition. You know you have properly internalized the mantra when you automatically use it in your dreams; when you are in the middle of a fearful nightmare and you intuitively free yourself by uttering the sacred phrase that instantly liberates you from the illusion... a very gratifying moment indeed. Of course the next step in this "dream yoga" is to realize that your "waking" life is equally ephemeral, and potentially free of fear and compulsion; this world too is a dream.

The universal mantra is OM, understood in the East for millennia as the primordial vibration. It is the Alpha and Omega of all creative sound, and it enervates all the human psychic energy centers. *OM is what the Universe says.*

RITUAL: MAKE IT SPECIAL

Ritual is symbolic self-reprogramming... special association for purposes of reminding us of the deeper levels and greater purpose for our being. Ritual can be an intelligent and often beautiful catalyst for expanded awareness. Examples include purification and cleansing rituals, lighting candles and incense, chanting, and performing sacred gestures such as bowing, symbolic of laying down the ego and honoring the greatness of God.

There are old rituals and new. You can inherit your tradition, be initiated into one, or design your own ceremonial rituals and invest them with meaning, so that whenever you return to them, they become potent catalysts for your greater purpose and identity.

PRAYER & DEVOTION

Prayer is better than sleep.

Islam

Prayer - a heart-centered path - is a way of working within the very convincing duality we perceive between ourselves and Divinity. It answers the challenge of our sense of finiteness with devotion and faith in the Infinite. It says, *I don't know it all, but that's okay, because I know You know.*

But if we see ourselves only as supplicants, as *lower* than the object of our prayers, we never *rise* to our own enlightenment. That very transformation is the answer to all prayer. *Instead of praying to Divinity, pray for Divinity!*

The prayer that liberates the soul is one of praise and partnership with God, not solicitation and expectations. The act of prayerful appreciation automatically connects you with the object of your devotion, whereas the assumption of need, and its implied dissatisfaction with existence, inherently disconnects.

FAITH AND HOW TO FIND IT

When thou passeth through the waters, I will be with thee, and through the rivers, they shall not over-flow thee; When thou walkest through fire, thou shalt not be burned; Neither shall the flame kindle upon thee.

Isaiah, 43

There comes a point when we must surrender and trust what we don't fully comprehend what's going on. When your theory doesn't hold water, and your boat is sinking fast. When you know that you don't know anything, and the pain is too great to bear.

Faith is when your parent or teacher or mate or child dies, and you're not ready or willing or able to handle the immense loss, but you must go on. Faith is saying "yes" to the Universe though it seems to be saying "no" to you. Faith helps when you get cancer, or AIDS, or some crippling or fatal disease. Faith is when you're having a baby, or healing, or crying, or dying, and it's definitely *not* in your control.

There is no formula for faith. It is hard-earned Grace. It comes when all else fails. It is the breakthrough of the soul. It proves that spirit goes on inexorably, within and without you. It allows you to jump off the cliff of your knowledge, and take flight on wings of unknown wisdom.

The mind creates the abyss -
The heart crosses it.

Nadar

VISUALIZATION:
SEEING YOUR WAY THROUGH

*But the kingdom of the Father is spread out upon the
earth, and men do not see it.*

Gospel of Thomas

Your imagination is one powerful tool. The problem is, most of us let our
imaginations run wild, and have no idea how (or even why) to train them. We
say "It's *only* your imagination," discounting the validity and creative essence of
the inner mind realm, while pursuing exclusively the sensory and the material.

The only difference between work and play, drudgery and joy, or - for that
matter - between disaster and opportunity, is one's attitude or *view*. Both the
content and the quality of experience depend on our predispositions. After all is
said and done, your reality begins and ends in your mind. Your world and
destiny emanate from your inner vision. What you get is what you project, and
what goes around comes around.

Positive thoughts can heal. "Terminal" cancer patients have boosted their
immune systems and increased their survival rates with regular visualization
practices. The key is clearly "seeing" the disease, the chosen therapy, and the
successful outcome in one's mind. *Paint a picture in your mind's eye of the
ailment, the cure in which you are investing your energy and belief, and the
desired results... Amazing things begin to happen: Helpful antibodies multiply
faster. Powerful hormones and trace compounds infuse the blood stream.
Organs are stimulated, and systems begin to balance. The mind-based approach
goes beyond the placebo effect, to auto-placebo: self-triggered (self-actuated)
healing.*

99

If you don't want to be in the dark,
let your light shine!

Elam

Suppose I tell you that the greatest revealed secret of esoteric mysticism is that you *can decide to be happy, immediately and permanently.* Even if at first you feel a momentary pleasant tingle, notice how your conditioned mind cannot help but respond with skepticism and rebuttals: *"Yes, but... "* Believe me, no matter how justified and sophisticated, it's that very automatic objection that keeps you unhappy (as well as unenlightened). Our very essence is ecstatic joy, but we perpetually postpone experiencing it, for lots of "good reasons." What's yours?

Think About It

All human potential is within. No accomplishment great or small, no ingenious invention, work of art, athletic achievement, or social advancement ever began as anything other than an idea in someone's head. My brain contains the only creative force at my disposal. Its evidence is the constant thought-stream of images reflected and projected in my mind. If my thoughts are cloudy and polluted, so will my life be. Conversely, clear, illuminated mind gives power to purpose.

Believe it. You can succeed and realize your dreams and never know defeat, by cultivating the latent powers of your own mind. You can achieve goals, manifest inventions, persuade adversaries, attract love, and heal yourself and others, if you only learn how to clearly and consistently "see" the desired outcome within the actual reality in which you find yourself. In positive visualization, you reconcile the actual and the possible, *first within your own mind.*

> *We will need to imagine ourselves as cells in a huge universal*
> *being who are in continual contact and cooperation with that*
> *Being's will. This will require a "mindless mind," an intellect*
> *which is more like a receiving mechanism rather than a*
> *thinking machine. The mind will become a receiver of inner*
> *impulses, rather than a thinker and decider. It will be a*
> *transformer of the oneness and beauty of our inner spiritual*
> *self into the material and mental worlds.*

Robert Najemy *Our Universal Self*

Picture This

You are in a tropical paradise, reclining on a beautiful white sand beach, under waying palm trees, admiring the expansive vista. The air is soothingly temperate nd scented with sea mist and intoxicating floral fragrances. As the immaculate hite surf rolls up and back over the sun-saturated shore, a fresh ocean breeze ently caresses your skin. Graceful birds hover in the distance. The sky is maculate blue. This is heaven on earth. You feel better than you have in a long me.

You notice someone approaching in the distance. Instinctively you recognize that is is an ally, a special friend. As this person draws near, you immediately feel even ore relieved and uplifted. Your eyes meet; you recognize the radiant being before u as your super-natural guide, smiling, as healing energy fills you. This is your uardian angel, your secret spiritual mentor.

You touch, then embrace your spirit guide, heart to heart. Intuitively, without esitation, you bond completely. Any last trace of doubt or fear melts away like sea am, replaced by a refreshing sense of all-knowing completion.

Your questions are answered, all your troubles dissolve, and you feel flooded with rofound understanding. You directly perceive the perfection of the universe. Your art is full of grace. A sense of timeless eternity allows you to become saturated ith deep peace. Then, as you silently emanate your gratitude, your spiritual friend egins to take leave. You bid a fond farewell, yet you know she/he will always be ere for you.

Without doubt your life has been changed positively. Your problems will never em quite as weighty, for you have received a "transmission," a glimpse of nlightenment, and it makes all the difference. Your own presence now becomes the ft to all those you will meet.

YOUR PSYCHIC ENERGY CENTERS

The world within is larger than the world outside.
Swami Rama

There is an ancient treasure map to the highest state of consciousness, and it is located as close as your own spinal column. Seven major landmarks along the way - the *chakras* - correspond to the stages of awakening through which we all eventually pass.

Chakra meditation is a kind of "Conscious Evolution." It accelerates soul growth by intentionally directing your energy into successively higher psychic centers. When all our centers are "open," we realize our full potential.

Wheels of Power

If you are alive, you are "wired" and charged with energy. Within you is a vast network of nerves which conduct electrical impulses between the central nervous system and the muscles, organs, glands, and sensory receptors throughout the body.

You are composed of trillions of cells, each holding a critical chemical balance of conductive minerals, insulating proteins, and electrolytic salts; each a potential receiver of these minute electro-chemical currents. In effect, every cell is a miniature living power plant, and several trillion of them, aligned and in circuit, generate the bio-electromagnetic energy field in which - and by which - you live and move. This life-energy is called "prana," in India, and "chi" in china. Mapping this internal circuitry, the Chinese evolved the healing art of acupuncture, which stimulates flow along energy "meridians."

The full three-dimensional emanation of all your energy is sometimes referred to as the "etheric body" or "aura." This highly active force field both reflects your state of health and responds to stimulation - a finding of some significance to medicine. It is a property of all living organisms, and is detectable with sensitive magnetometers, infra-red sensors, Kirlian photography, and other scanning devices. This energy is the creative force and vital sustainer of the physical body, and connects it with mind and emotions.

The physical "wiring" for human bio-energy is the central nervous system. We now know that it is not exclusively an *automatic* system. Biofeedback technology shows what the ancient eastern body/mind science of yoga has known for ages: with training and practice, the energies in the body can be sensed, harnessed, enhanced, and directed.

The Sanskrit word "chakra" means "wheel." The chakras within the human energy field are vortices of life force, where it concentrates like sunlight through a lens. Chakras are located in various places within the body, including the palms and the soles of the feet, but the seven most significant occur along the length of the spine. They are depicted in the medical symbol, the Caduceus, as the crossing points of two rising snakes, the positive and negative energy currents. These energy foci are not anatomical structures, though they do correspond to various glands.

The "yoga" or "internal science" of opening the energy centers has endured for five thousand years, because it works! Chakra meditation is experience-based, not theoretical or magical. With specific, systematic mind/body techniques, you can induce or accelerate functional improvements in various organs and glands, as well as positive, psycho-spiritual growth.

Aside from their organic relevance, each chakra represents a psychologically different way of perceiving reality, and interacting with the world. We can think of the chakras as "sub-personalities," or stages of development. Furthermore, human evolution itself embodies our progression through these stages, from primal to Divine. Chakra meditation refines the nervous system and induces spiritual development.

For example, yogis have said that in most people today, the pineal gland is a dormant organ, waiting for the appropriate higher mental energies necessary to activate and utilize it. Its sixth-chakra functions may have something to do with "non-ordinary" states - peak experiences, telepathy and pre-cognition - experiences often reported after extended practice of chakra/energy meditation.

It is not even necessary at the outset to "believe" in the chakras in order to make good use of the chakra visualization approach. Because the subtle human energies involved respond readily to thought, you merely have to *imagine* that you are feeling them in the appropriate locations. They soon become self-evident. This is because no experience can be "just in your imagination." *Every mental event has a physical correlate.* This has profound implications for self-healing, and chakra meditation creates particularly reliable, positive psycho-somatic effects.

Through careful application of core relaxation techniques, breath awareness exercises, imagery, and intonation, an inner stream of concentrated energy is released upwards through the central channel of the spine. Thus, the seven chakras can be conceived as psychic valves - though they cannot be forcibly opened. (They are also frequently depicted as flowers).

Chakra visualization complements other stress-reduction and auto-regulation techniques. As with all effective self-development strategies, regular practice is a pre-requisite for quality results. The enhancement of one's well-being will be deep and lasting in proportion to the commitment to the method.

YOUR JOURNEY THROUGH THE CHAKRAS

The following guided meditation is designed to be heard while sitting still, in a quiet, receptive state. Although simply reading it can be quite useful, the best strategy is to pre-record the narrative on tape, or have someone with a soothing, natural voice read it to you.[4] You can also gaze at the colored symbols in the Chakra Meditation chart during the narration.

The ideal location for meditation is private, neat, warm, well-ventilated, quiet and softly lit. The body should be clean and relaxed, clothing loose and comfortable, with plenty of breathing room. Close the door, disconnect the phone, light a candle, perhaps some incense. Spend a few moments doing your favorite stretches, then sit down, take a few deep breaths, and relax.

It does not matter whether you sit on the floor or on a chair, so long as your knees are lower than your hips, your spine is upright and balanced, and you can breathe freely. Get all your fidgeting and adjusting done first. Find the most comfortable, balanced, relaxed sitting position you can, and prepare to release your body and still your mind for deep meditation.

---

[4] For a CD of the author reading <u>Journey Through the Chakras</u>, send $19 to: ENLIGHTENMENT PROJECTS 121-F Old Town Farm Rd., Peterborough, NH 03458.

Chakra Meditation

Chakra	Element	Color	Symbol	Sensation Location	Power	Feel Your
CROWN	space	violet		frontal lobe, pituitary gland, fontanel, aura	infinite wisdom, god unity	divinity
THIRD EYE	spirit	indigo		eyes, cerebral cortex,	intuition, telepathy, extra sensory perception	spirituality
THROAT	ether	blue		mouth, tongue, throat, neck ears	self-expression, communication	creativity
HEART	air	green		heart, lungs, chest, arms, hands	love, compassion sacrifice soul union	empathy
NAVEL	fire	yellow		belly, diaphragm, breath, stomach	protection, control, conquest	power, strength
SEX	water	orange		sex center, reproductive glands, pelvis, buttocks, legs	physical union procreation	desire, passion
ROOT	earth	red		coccyx, anus, feet	primal animal survival instincts	body

Guided Visualization

As you sit erect, spine aligned to the earth's center, envision a vertical double helix of vibrant energy embracing and dancing around your spinal column, magnetizing and polarizing its hollow core. One spiral comes down from above and infuses dense matter with the spirit of life. The other spiral draws the power of the earth up to meet the light above your head. Your whole body is a reflection of the balance and play of these two powerful energies, flowing and glowing, between the magnetic poles of your spine.

ROOT CHAKRA

Take a deep breath and pull it down through your body to the very base of your spine, the seat of the first chakra. As you release the air, relax all the muscles in your toes, feet and legs. Take in more air and focus on your connecting points to the earth. Now release the air, .. relax down through your body, and continue to send your attention deep into the center of the earth. Picture magnetic lines of force coming from the earth's core, connecting with your own root center. Allow that force to arise within you, from below.

Imagine a feeling of power surging into this "root" center from the deep center of the earth. As it increases, keep your attention on this powerful magnetic energy at the end of your spine.

Imagine that with each breath, energy collects and builds at your base. Continue to relax, and sense the feelings in the coccyx, perineum, anus, and deep inside your pelvic cavity, the foundation of your body. Sensing your root center, breathe as if the earth's energy is coming directly into you from below. Allow the energy to build, like a growing, magnetic force.

Feel the weight of your attachment to the earth: its gravitational pull on your body, through the mass of.. dirt.. clay.. minerals.. rock and magma. Sense the whole planet's mass under you, pulling you down towards dense earth. You are born of this earth, and when you die, your body will return to it.

Earth animal that you are, you eat of the earth and eliminate earth fertilizer. Your awareness is purely biological, immersed in life's survival imperative and ecological cycles. In the womb of creation, you are pulsating flesh, bound by living sinews and fibers. The dominant color is blood red. Smell your own odors. Feel the cool dirt.

Be aware of your pelvic area, legs, and feet. Feel the density of your bones, the core and support structure of your body, minerals taken up from the earth and deposited inside you, compacted by gravity, formed against the force of the earth.

You are at the most primitive stage of evolution. Your behavior is animal-instinctual and reactive. You are motivated by survival drives, such as hunger and fear. You are isolated and fiercely individual. All you know of reality is physical and self-referent. Like an infant, you identify solely with the body, and exist in a sensory, material realm of stimulus and response. You experience yourself at the center of everything that happens. You love to eat and sleep. You fear pain and death.

Your sole purpose is self-preservation. Persistent and self-sufficient, you can be greedy or aggressive. Allow yourself to acknowledge this "dark" side, and your potential for "small- mindedness," for it is the necessary lesson of this level of existence. Know yourself as an inheritor of animal instincts, and primitive tendencies. Fully accept that you are a creature of habits and needs, rooted in the earth.

Continuing to breathe in and out through your lowest nerve plexus, allow your body to begin to feel that you are in a safe place. Perhaps you feel secure and comfortable enough to let go of your protection.. to relax, and sigh. You could use the affirmation. "I belong on this earth." (repeat..) or "Here and now, I feel safe." (repeat..)

As your breath pulls up the Earth's energy, picture at your root center a red square box, filled with dark, rich soil which is moist and cool. Inside, a coiled serpent is sleeping... Your task is to warm the environment, and so wake up the snake.

SECOND CHAKRA: LIBIDO

Keeping the first chakra open, take a long deep breath in, and lift your awareness from your root center, up to the second chakra, the area of your sexual and reproductive organs. Take in more, letting the red energy from below heat up to a glowing orange surge... Now let the air rush out and begin to consciously relax your genital muscles, buttocks, abdomen, hips, and pelvis. Breathe the warm energy into the second chakra, deep inside your sexual center. Allow the power generated below to surge upwards and spread out at this second energy level, like warm, orange lava flowing out of a powerful volcano.

As each breath washes through your pelvic cavity, notice your desires awakening. Moisture softens the earth., it becomes fluid, and the energy of movement develops. Things smell juicy, and you want a taste.

This is the level of sensation, attraction, physical pleasure. It's also the center of regeneration and procreation. Sense the womb or gonads as well as the vagina or penis. Feel into the very center of your sex. Imagine that each breath you take sensitizes and charges this second level energy center, your reproductive and sexual stimulation plexus.

Breathe freely through the second chakra as if drawing energy up from the earth, feeling the surge as you release any residual tightness from the genital muscles, anus, buttocks, thighs, and down your legs. Tune into any sense of warmth or vibration, and allow it to grow and surge, while breathing and centering on this sexual-pro-creative power within you, the most powerful biological force in the universe. At this time and place, give in to the urge to feel it totally. Feel the pleasure-pressure in your groin and glands.

The natural element is water; it is mutable and not easily contained. You are pulled by the moon, and swayed by emotional tides. You are in the ocean and you are of the ocean. The sea is all around you, as the blood stream permeates you within. Your internal sea of blood bathes the trillions of cells in your body. They swim in a rich warm primal soup of salty, boyant nutrients.

Here, the human evolutionary stage is primal/procreative. You are dominated by desire and the powerful urge for physical gratification, driven by the polarity of attraction and repulsion.

Accept your own physical needs and pleasures. You are a sexual being surrounded by sexual beings. All of creation is sexy. You can delight in the stimulation of energy, color, gorgeous forms.

Your sexual powers can imprison or liberate. Sex can reinforce the small self and the illusion of separation, or it can be a gateway to mystical union with the beloved. In the exquisite paradox of creation, your body both entraps and frees you.

Receive and celebrate the gift of your sensuality, and the irresistible vibrations and rhythms of life. Know yourself as a sexual being, with outer attractiveness and inner personal powers. Open to your own animal magnetism, and the ingenious genetic desire system that keeps our species reproducing.

Picture an upward facing, glowing orange crescent inside you, with the very center where you feel your procreative energy most concentrated and alive. Feel the vibrating magnetic energy pulsate in your sex center.

As you breathe more deeply through the second chakra, think of your need for others, and your potential for desire for love within your animal form. Imagine yourself feeling healthy sexual stimulation. To be totally opened in your second chakra, embrace your object of desire with complete passion and abandonment. Make love in meditation. Open the pleasure center completely.

(Momentarily dip back down to the first chakra, and make sure it is fully open by relaxing your feet, legs, and buttocks on an exhalation. Breathing in, come back up and do the same at the second level, relaxing the genital and rectal muscles, and opening to the upward flow of your energy.)

THIRD CHAKRA: POWER

Now take a deeper inhalation and lift your awareness to the third chakra, the abdominal/solar plexus center in your belly. While exhaling, let your attention settle here in your middle, your center of gravity. The color changes from orange to fire yellow,

Imagine that your breath comes not through your nose, but directly into your belly. Feel the air flowing into your gut. As you meditate on this glowing power center, sense the force within your diaphragm that moves your breath in and out automatically. Allow that innate rhythm free range to determine the depth and pace of your breathing, and feel how it gently affects the surrounding areas. Continue letting all your stomach muscles relax deeper, and feel the entire diaphragm itself relaxing, particularly on exhalations.

The third chakra governs the pancreas and adrenal glands, and the stomach, intestines, the kidneys, gall bladder, and the diaphragm. Feel these organs inside you. This "solar plexus" energy center controls breathing and digestion, as oxygen and nutrients catalyze and release your body heat.

The belly center ("hara" in Japanese) is your gravitational center and the source of your personal power. It is linked to your body's "fight or flight" mechanism, and reflects your moment to moment dynamics with the outside world: whether you feel vulnerable or trusting; in control or afraid. If you fear - if you are anxious, defensive, or aggressive - it shows up as abdominal tightness and restricted breathing.

So, tell your body that you are in a safe, secure place, and let your belly become as soft as a defenseless baby's. Every time you let out a breath, release all muscle tension, along with all remaining negative or protective feelings.

Your belly is the center of control and trust. At the "gut level" we learn to discriminate between friend and foe, distress and exhilaration, and to respond accordingly. From this center you laugh or cry. Both are equally necessary.

The color is flame yellow. The energy from below is warming up. Picture a glowing ember being fanned hotter with each breath you take, until a flame appears. Feel the radiant heat from within.

Now you begin to see more of the world and its possibilities. You have discovered others as something more than food or threat or sex object. You are developing a social personality. You want the security of belonging. You become concerned with family, territory, politics. You begin to use your will power to affect your environment.

Know yourself as a social being, engaging others as partners and allies, and sometimes, enemies. You can fight for what you want, or compromise for mutual benefit. Now you can sublimate your primal instincts, postpone instant gratification, and instead make and pursue plans goals.

You have the capacity to experience doubt, fear, and inhibition, but you can also be altruistic and heroic. Ambition arises; for status and wealth... yet you can surrender your egocentric view by finding a larger group to give your allegiance, like your family, church, community, or nation. Your behavior is determined by cultural dynamics.

The dangers of this level are self-righteousness and aggression, but you are also learning the value of self-control.

Breathe power into your hara\belly center. Imagine you are lost in a jungle... confused and afraid. Suddenly a cleared path appears before you. The path leads to a cave inside a mountain. In the center of the cave is a fire. Now you recognize your mission is to keep the fire from dying out or raging out of control.

FOURTH CHAKRA : LOVE

Take another slightly deeper inhalation and draw your attention up to the center of your chest. Take in more. As you exhale, settle your awareness on this heart center, and imagine it feeling stronger, while at the same time reopening all previous levels in succession.

The fourth chakra rules the adrenal glands, kidneys, heart and lungs. The native element is air, and the feelings are light and expansive. The color is emerald green, natures own color of life, nourishment, and healing.

The transition from third to fourth chakra is a major evolutionary step, and one that differentiates man from pure animal nature. Here, you have the potential for looking beyond your personal ego and melodrama, achieving some sense of balance between yourself the greater world.

This is the center of the higher functions of love, compassion, empathy, forgiveness and self-sacrifice. Here we become conscious participants in our own evolution. The heart is the center of the true calling of all human souls: pure unconditional love.

In your heart, you integrate body, mind and emotions. The outer and inner lives are in dynamic equilibrium. You work more patiently with the duality of things. You discover that mutual cooperation is better than fighting. Your boundaries begin to get softer, and you love it.

The symbol is the six-pointed star, the confluence of the downward and upward power triangles. Fully human, you are halfway between earth and heaven. In the heart chakra, you have the opportunity to choose to live and work for more than mere personal survival. You discover some principles worth living and dying for.

You can open your heart to others. This begins with taking pleasure in the happiness of loved ones, and evolves, through community service, and ecological awareness, to the direct experience of the larger bodies of beings in which we participate, including the Earth Herself. For the Earth is the heart center of the Solar System.

At the heart, your main motivators are love, compassion, harmony, peace, and cooperation. There is a sense of the interconnectedness of all beings, and a deep, somewhat saddened perception of the prevalence of unnecessary suffering in the world. With an open heart, you learn the higher qualities of goodwill, altruism, devotion, and sacrifice. Now team success is at least as important as personal success.

Fourth chakra energy makes you a natural gardener, good cook, skillful parent and a compassionate mate. You are capable of feeling religious. With love, you can teach and even heal others. You feel life's full complement of human emotions - from grief to joy - and somehow contain it all in a humane and workable way.

If the belly is the center of control, the Heart is the center of the loss-of-control: laughter, the emotional equivalent of orgasm. Both laughter and orgasm are kinds of ego-death. When we let loose with uncontrollable laughter, the rigid personality loses hold, excess tension is dissipated, and the protection mechanism is reset to zero. When you laugh, you unblock the emotional center, and fill the heart. (Spiritually, the best thing to laugh about is yourself.)

Breathe in a relaxed manner, through your heart center, and imagine your beloved appearing before you. Just feel the love coming in and out of your heart with each breath. You can picture colored light beams, or symbolic images, like streams of little cartoon valentines streaming between you. Feel your most gentle, generous nature emerge, as when a mother nurses her infant. Breathe in soothing love (remind yourself that you too deserve to receive some of the beneficial loving vibrations in the world) and give it away every time you exhale. See your loved one sitting before you receiving all this most excellent, healing love energy. Wrap your beloved in a glowing mantle of your highest esteem and most caring love.

Now allow your envelope of love to grow to include all the people you know, then and all the people you don't know, until your expanding love covers the world, and you feel boundless compassion for all sentient beings in your heart.

Let each exhalation begin by relaxing you physically, and end by opening you spiritually, like a flower unfolding its petals. Know yourself as a kind, generous, loving human being of goodwill, worthy of giving and receiving the unconditional love that renews the soul. Pray for the welfare of us all.

FIFTH CHAKRA: CREATIVITY

Now inhale somewhat forcefully and pull all that energy up from the deep red root center, through the orange sexual/regenerative center, and up and through the yellow power plexus, and the green heart level, and into your throat area, which is a beautiful deep blue color. Hold the air and energy in for a moment while relaxing... take in more. Now relax and soften your tongue, vocal cords, epiglottis, neck muscles, shoulders, arms and hands. With each exhalation, feel the radiant energy in your thyroid at the base of the neck, and throughout your entire upper respiratory tract. Sigh out the sound, "ahhh.." Open the throat chakra.

The image is an open chalice. The color is royal blue. The element is the subtle, highly vibrating etheric. And the human sense is pure thought. In the throat chakra we discover the true power of intention.

The throat chakra is the seat of personal creativity, and self-healing. The thyroid is a master regulator of the other endocrine glands and many of the body's complex metabolic systems, hormonal balances and immune functions. Send the message from your mind to your body that all systems may now be in perfect equilibrium.

Visualize crystal blue light shining through your neck and throat, clearing out all constriction. Let go of all tension, and relax from the jaw and tongue to the throat, neck and shoulders, and replace it with feelings of open space.

The "voice" center mediates your communication skills, your artistic sense, your use of tools and complex systems, and your capacity for innovation. Know yourself as a sensitive, creative being, with an original contribution to make in the world.

The throat chakra is the origin of our thought-forms, which bear real force in the world. A "word" is a creative union of thought and energy.. a vibration with purpose and meaning, utilizing the primacy of idea and sound in creation. "In the beginning was the WORD and the word was with God." At this level, ideas become thoughts, concepts, language.. and your plans take on the energy to manifest in the world, as the actual results of your intent and skill. As Peter Pan said: Think good thoughts!

If you are blocked in the voice center, you may have trouble being heard, or feel inept or unoriginal. To overcome obstructions in this creative center, deliberately replace all your negative ideas about yourself with positive ones. Say internally, "I am truly effective and creative."

The medium of the mind in the voice is higher thought, and symbolic knowledge. Fifth chakra dynamics are subtle, philosophical, poetic, and reflective. Consciously invoke your sense of purpose, and highest personal aspirations. Bring to mind the example and inspiration of teachers and saints. As you physically and psychically "open" your throat center, know yourself as a creative person, with an innate ability to speak the truth effectively, respond authentically to ideas, and to create and appreciate Beauty itself.

As you feel your breath pass through your throat, sigh out the sound "Ahhh.." Picture a pure crystal chalice filled with brilliant, deep blue light. Out of the center, a beautiful white dove emerges, spreads her wings, and lifts into the sky with breathtaking grace. You feel blessed by the vision.

SIXTH CHAKRA: INTUITION

With the throat chakra remaining open, take a deeper breath in, and lift your awareness to the psychic center between your eyebrows, in the middle of your forehead. Then relax deeply and imagine that each breath has the effect of opening this "Third Eye" center, like a window opening to a morning sunrise. Allow the brilliant light directly into your forehead center, splashing a rainbow of color through your brain. You feel your head getting more transparent. Now picture a radiant super-natural indigo light flooding in through your eyes and head, illuminating your consciousness in all directions and dimensions.

Focus on your senses of seeing and hearing. Now realize their psychic dimension: that of inner vision, and hearing the "still, silent voice" of intuition. Tune into your pineal gland, seated deep behind your eyes, just under the forebrain. It's like a tiny radio transceiver. Imagine that by settling into deep meditative perception, you can simply and easily turn on your higher functions: intuition, clairvoyance, telepathy, precognition- your ability to know beyond the limits of your senses. The color is indigo violet, the vibratory ray of spiritual mastership.

At the sixth chakra - the inner eye center - you have the potential to rise above your separate, personal identity altogether. Here the essential motivators are Truth, Divine Love, and direct perception of the great unseen forces that shape our world and universe. Absolute selflessness enables you to see beyond the ordinary limits of time and space. Your far-reaching knowledge is not a matter of belief, but one of living experience.

Let in through the open window of the inner eye, the universal Light that dispels all darkness, all dis-ease, and doubt. Know yourself as a highly evolved soul, reincarnating through this and many other lives, on a cosmic journey towards Enlightenment. Your mission is to liberate yourself and others from delusion and the pain it causes.

Tune in to the world telepathically; perceiving both the dense and subtle levels of reality. Your third eye is like an x-ray laser beam, probing the astral field, the deeper soul-levels of life, seeing the connecting patterns, the underlying universal energy, and the meaning of things. You begin to perceive the Divine connection, and you stand in reverence and awe.

You rediscover your gifts of healing, true dreaming, and spontaneous teaching. You know how to use soul force, and you attract power by giving it away. You can create an atmosphere of serenity at will. The only lesson you have to learn here is the truly infinite nature of your own being.

Look into the deep black space, boundless and empty. Contemplate the potential power of pure consciousness..

You are like an eagle, with keen vision, and regal vantage point. From here, you see that all is connected and united. The world is a shimmering sphere suspended in the space of your mind. Its transformation results from your heightened positive intent, linked with millions of people of goodwill throughout the globe.

SEVENTH CHAKRA: ENLIGHTENED

Breathe in, and come up. Hold it.. Release. The crown chakra.. It is like a thousand-petaled lotus opening upward from the top of your head. This "fontanel" is where you enter and exit the physical body as a soul evolving through numberless incarnations.

The glands are the pituitary and thalamus, deep in the brain. The color is luminous super-natural violet, reaching up to the brilliant white of pure cosmic consciousness itself.

In the throat center, you are knowledge. In the eyebrow center you are intuition. In the crown you are wisdom. You see beyond birth and death. Here are the laws of creation revealed. You know the universality of awareness that transcends the small self and the material world. You perceive on the super-conscious level, and everything is Divine, Infinite, Spiritual.. including the very one and only Self, the Living Spirit of the Universe.

Beyond language and concepts, insight is complete, understanding vast. There is no difference between creation and creator. You are fully conscious of your part in the manifestation of reality, in the constant re-creation of this world, and the sustenance of the precious physical vehicle, your body. Fullness and emptiness are the same; nothing is lacking, and there's nothing to do but be. Bliss is a fundamental truth of existence. The Universe is your home. You are none other than the Ancient One, the pure and full Awareness of God. Nothing is required of this One.

Here is Enlightenment- not some thing to attain, but what you already are in essence: master of body, mind, and emotions, karma, and destiny. You realize your birthright, the bliss of re-absorption into the Universe, even in this very body. Spiritually, there are no needs. A perfect instrument of the Great Plan, you effortlessly contribute to the evolution of humanity and the planet towards Enlightenment. You are fulfilling this destiny, right now.

All colors together become white. An iridescent fountain of pure, brilliant white energy surges up from the earth, through your root center. You feel it stimulate your glands, warm your belly, fill your heart, resonate in your voice, vibrate your ears, eyes and brain, and shoot out the top of your head - a brilliant white fountain of pure universal energy - shining from your head into the sky and deep space beyond.

You are a wide open conduit, free and open at every level. You expand your awareness over and around the physical body, remaining connected to the source, and centered in the world.

As you breathe freely, you know yourself as a pure channel transmitting (and transmuting) energy between earth and heaven, in perfect balance and equanimity. You are full of potential power, yet totally comfortable within this center of silence.

A pure and perfect, highly polished, extremely hard diamond crystal rests in the center of a delicately beautiful, soft pink lotus flower in full blossom. Spontaneously intuiting the union of these two forms, knowing is now from the crown chakra level..

You have traveled long and far, from darkness, fear, and total isolation, through the development of interpersonal relationships and discovery of the world, and ever-expanding dimensions, ever finer states of awareness, until you finally realize your connection - indeed your identity with -the whole of the Universe. Remain open at all levels, and savor in the silence the experience of knowing your true Self, as infinite, whole and holy.

Lonny J. Brown

DREAMS ARE RELATIVELY REAL

*Everything there is to know about God
is already written on your heart.*

In the dream state the vast and mysterious reservoir of the subconscious touches awareness unimpeded by socialized filters or conditioned belief. Our dreams speak to us in symbolic scenarios of alternate realities, bypassing intellectual and ego defenses. Dream symbols are the mystical language of submerged wisdom calling to become known. "Pleasant dreams" are epiphanies of insight into the self-liberating nature of mind. "Nightmares" are the fear and guilt we need to acknowledge.

Sharing and interpreting dreams in tribal, familial, or professional settings can be therapeutic and enlightening. Thus dreaming becomes awakening.

Conscious dreaming is accomplished by bringing one's awake presence of mind into the sleep state so as to fully realize the projected nature of the mind-based scenario. It requires meditative mind-training to maintain continuity of awareness going into "subconsciousness." The experience liberates one from the vicissitudes of the dream drama, and bestows the creative power of director on the dreamer. Of course, the real point of such "dream yoga" is to apply it to one's regular waking state; our everyday "reality" is also a dream, and waking up to the "meta-real" requires the very same self-realizing presence of mind.

116

THERAPY AS CONSCIOUS EVOLUTION

*No one is ever away from the Self, and therefore
everyone is in fact self-realized. Only - and this is the
great mystery - people do not know this and want to
realize the Self... realization consists only in getting rid of
the false idea that one is not realized*

Ramana Maharshi

Western psychotherapy is designed to restore a healthy sense of self.
Meditation and spiritual practices take it from there, towards ego-transcendence
(sometimes called "higher Self"). The new integral humanistic, transpersonal
and Buddhist schools of psychology include spirituality and transformation as
part of mental health. Enlightenment and sanity coincide.

Therapy is only as good as your therapist. The best counselors are secretly
enlightened spiritual healers. They can help you see your neurotic blind spots,
integrate all aspects of the psyche, remember your innate basic sanity and
goodness, and connect with the Universal. Ideally it's a journey of self-discovery
and transformation, guided by someone who's been there.

117

SACRED SUBSTANCES: The Flesh of the Gods

OK, now for a trick question.. and don't be too quick to assume you know the answer...
Can mind-expanding drugs foster Enlightenment?

For ages, cultures indigenous to every continent on earth have been using powerful mind-altering plants to foster religious and mystical experience. Accounts abound of initiates and native shamen ingesting peyote cactus, psilocybin mushrooms, or other potent mind-altering organic substances to heal and be healed, to achieve knowledge, and enter into transcendent states. Could this all amount to nothing more than primitive delusion and self-deception?

Serious, qualified scholars and researchers such as R.E.L. Masters, Jean Houston, Stanislov Groff, Alan Watts, Andrew Weil, Aldous Huxley and William James have upheld the legitimacy of these religious sacraments, at least within their traditional contexts. In a bold and now-famous experiment conducted in 1962 at Harvard University Divinity School, Dr. Walter Pahnke administered high dosages of the traditional Native American psychoactive sacrament psilocybin to ten theology students at a Good Friday service. His triple-blind experiment included a control group of another ten students, receiving placebos. The result has come to be known as *The Miracle of March Chapel.*

As reported in Masters and Houston's *The Varieties of Psychedelic Experience,* "nine subjects from the psilocybin group reported having religious experiences which they considered to be genuine. Only one of the placebo subjects also claimed to have experienced phenomena of a religious nature."

In a similar experiment, Dr. Timothy Leary arranged for sixty-nine full-time religious professionals to ingest psilocybin in a supportive setting. Over seventy-five percent of these subjects stated that they had experienced "intense mystico-religious reactions, and considerably more than half claim that they have had the deepest spiritual experience of their life."[5]

---

[5] More recently, (2006) researchers at Johns Hopkins University found that more than 60 percent of the subjects who received hallucinogenic psilocybin mushrooms in a controlled experiment had a

But if spirituality is available from funny fungi and wacky weeds, why aren't the millions of tripped-out hippies and psychedelic pilgrims who have indulged since the sixties all obviously happy and holy? Why can't we just prescribe enough LSD for everyone to halt all brutality and war, and create a heaven on earth, as was so naively asserted by the young mystics of their day?[6]

The answer can be summed up in one word: predisposition. *Where you go depends on where you're coming from.* Inevitably - as decades of experimentation with "recreational" drugs have proven - the outcome depends on the input.

These powerful substances are not themselves a source of inspiration, insight, wisdom or anything else. They merely act as mirrors and magnifying lenses, through which we see our own mind-set: our inclinations, desires, aspirations, expectations, and fears. This explains why one man's sacrament can be another man's poison: it depends on your intention and training (or lack of it). In mind-states as in info-tech, it's definitely a case of *garbage in, garbage out.*

For those in the habit of relating to life with respect, psychotropic drugs only enhance their reverence for the awesome majesty all around. Not surprisingly, if a person's mind is a mess, such will be their LSD trip. If your quest is altruistic, your chosen sacraments will serve to expand your compassion and understanding. If you are enamored with your own little reality and drama, you may find yourself in a hall of mirrors with no exit.

So, is there instant Enlightenment? Yes and No. Whether through discipline, devotion, karma, faith or grace... the rarefied atmosphere of ultimate understanding that loosens the bonds of ordinary reality and dissolves the ego might occur through psycho-active bio-chemicals as with any other powerful catalyst. But the mentally lazy or deluded will hardly recognize the revelation, no matter what may be introduced into body or brain. That's why training and rituals evolved over thousands of years to protect both the native people and the power of their chosen sacraments.

The living spirit is nowhere to be found if not within your own heart. When it awakens, everything becomes sacred, and you are transformed by the power of this realization.

---

self-described "complete mystical experience," and ranked it as one of the most spiritually significant events in their lives.

[6] Legend has it that in the 60's, the great beat poet Alan Ginsberg once dropped acid and tried calling the White House to get President Nixon to try it!

Lonny J. Brown

WHAT'S LOVE GOT TO DO WITH IT?

Space is for the extension of Love.
Time is for the evolution of Love.
Matter is for the expression of Love.
Eternity is for the living of Love.

Claude Curling, physicist

If my eyes are open but my heart is closed,
I will never know the true path.

Nadar

Love makes the world go 'round. Love is the glue of the Universe, the very attraction that keeps every electron of every atom in orbit around it's own nucleus, and coalesces billion-light-year wide galaxies.

On the human level, conscious, unconditional love is one good indicator that enlightenment is near. True love is the nemesis of the ego: it places the beloved before self. The selfish ego gives its own requirements the exalted name of Love. It says, "I love you," and means "I need you," or "I want you," or "I'll love you, if..." True love delights in serving the beloved, even invisibly.

Real Love anticipates and fulfills the needs of the other. The word "sacrifice" comes from "sacred fire." Can you burn up your self-importance at the sacrificial alter of Love?. Sacred Love sanctifies the lover with compassion, tenderness, and infinite patience. Conscious spiritual marriage is among the highest of yogas.

Your love may begin locally, but Enlightened Love never knows where to stop. You may be introduced to it by your affections for a puppy or a child. It may then transfer to a lover, mate, family, and friends. But to be enlightening, your love must continue, embracing an ever-wider family of loved ones, until you realize its scope covers all life. For Big Love shines omni-directionally, and indiscriminately like the sun. It warms all beings, great and small, without assessing their worthiness. Love is God's middle name.

120

EMPTY YOUR SELF

Avoid losing your life.. Give it away.

Elam

Here is the closest thing to a formula for Enlightenment you'll find in this book: *Give your self away.* Which is of course easier said than done (not to mention thoroughly open to misinterpretation).

Erase Old Tapes

Forgiveness is the first servant of Love. Can we forgive ourselves for past transgressions, and others as we would little children their innocent offenses? Expand your sense of compassion to absolve old grudges, even for the most egregious offenders. What does bitterness do for you? Have you actually tried loving your enemy? Find hatred within and scrutinize it out of existence. If it takes a lifetime, you must persist. Baptize yourself in forgiveness and find Universal Love.

All you have to do is find a principle worth dying for, and live for it instead. Christianity has the *Imitation of Christ.* In Buddhism the Bodhisattva dedicates him/herself to enlightenment for the sake of all sentient beings. Everyone you meet becomes your brother/sister/mother/lover/master/child. You turn yourself inside-out and make everyone's happiness your conscious intention. In this way we come to live the truth of the interconnectedness of all.

And old spiritual adage holds that if you make a list of all the possessions and problems you call "mine," the extent of that list equals how far you are from heaven. The quickest (albeit hottest) bypass of this long distance is to mentally burn everything on the list, to stand naked before the world, and offer the Universe unconditional surrender, as devotee, lover, servant of all life.

Service does not mean unworthiness and subservience to others, but rather the actual egolessness of the realized spirit. This is super-natural magic. *You become the Universe by "unbecoming" your self.* Embrace that which you would have avoided, and instantly transform every obstacle into an opportunity. This is the "secret" of the magical/alchemical transformation of ego into enlightenment.

Lonny J. Brown

ENLIGHTENMENT ONLINE

We are merging - as a global economy, society and entity - into a Living Matrix which in many ways resembles a real-time "global neural network." This "neural network" is the marriage of global mind, body and spirit. Each of its components is working in tandem with the other to send and receive information that spans the globe through the neural-net software of the Virtual Tao.

Alexander Besher, Pamela Engebretson, & Francoise Bollerot:
Global House: A 21st Century Meditation

The "Global Village" predicted by 60's media philosopher Marshal McLuhan is now upon us, thanks to cable TV, satellite-relayed phone networks, computerized libraries, and the final wiring job for the planetary electronic nervous system, the Internet. While the world is shrinking, our collective awareness is expanding, as the great new knowledge repository of Cyberspace mushrooms exponentially in size and scope.

Some observers feel we are witnessing an evolutionary quantum leap in human consciousness, heralding the emergence of the transpersonal level of awareness termed the "Noosphere," by French mystic Pierre Teilard de Chardin, and the Global Brain by contemporary author Peter Russell. Whatever we call the new omni-dimension of human awareness and interaction, it seems that the salient question now is, how can we best utilize Cyberspace to serve the Earth's sustenance and humankind's enlightenment?

What is the meaning, significance, and highest potential value of the new electronic omnisphere? How can the digital global nerve network be used to communicate real wisdom, and to advance a vision of our best possibilities? I believe that the multi-dimensional link-up we are undergoing amounts to nothing less than the next step in the evolution of human consciousness and the emerging self-awareness of the Planetary Mind. Many forward-thinkers are convinced that the Internet and the World Wide Web can be a vitally important force for personal transformation, community building, enlightened participatory democracy, environmental protection, and planetary salvation. Do you agree? How can the Internet help *you* in your personal quest for spiritual realization, and how can we all help make this enlightened vision of Cyberspace a reality?

122

PRAYER OF A CYBERNAUT

Are You out there, Lord, just waiting for us to realize once again and in a whole new way, your absolute imminence and omnipresence?

Is your cosmic energy behind the millions of hooked-up hackers, bleary-eyed cubicle dwellers, students viewing cyber-porn, working single mothers getting e-mail support, buzz-cut cyberpunks publishing outrageous electronic anti-'zines from their bedrooms and basements?

How about the countless neurotic wanderers, frustrated dreamers, lost lovers, false prophets and true believers lurking just beyond my screen, wandering the endless byways of the digisphere? Is that You too, oh Great Creator, in disguise, teaching us yet again how to meet and get along on another level, how to learn to love and accept and help our brothers and sisters on-line, as in that other holographic projection we call "real" life?

"The medium is the message," said the Prophet.. So what is the Internet? Will it at long last fulfill the promise of an enlightened humanity, or signal only increasing culture clash, commercial exploitation, and the dumbing down of the mass mind? Can we really construct a modern info-super-high-way for the coming generation that serves all and sets us free, or is it destined to become the next wasteland, full of needless junk, violence, mindless distractions and untold cost?

If "you are that which you seek" is the computerized planetary virtual world an extension of my mind? Where does "my" mind end and "our" mind begin, in the shared everywhere of Cyberspace? If and when we find out, what should we do about it?

Teach me, Lord, to see Your All-Dimensional Interface behind this flat-screen display, to hear Your multi-media message of Truth, to download Your divine program, to know Your timeless omnipresence within the vast, pulsating electrodynamic universe, to become a fully-conscious participant in Your earthly energy body/mind. Amen

DOES THE INTERNET HAVE
BUDDHA NATURE?

True to Buddhism's long history of openness and ready adaptation to different cultures, the online Buddhist community is embracing the new digital-etheric network most enthusiastically.

No doubt one reason why Buddhists feel so at home in the invisible yet all-pervasive realm of the Internet is their understanding of the ephemeral nature of the material world. Long before nuclear physicists confirmed that matter is actually energy, and that energy in turn is *no thing*, Buddhists were meditating on the non-substantiality of existence, also known as *Sunyata* and often translated as "emptiness" or "void." Cyberspace is no more real or unreal, important or unimportant, than the "reality" we inhabit all the time. It is another *loka*, a level of transient psychological incarnation. Just like the human and heaven and hell realms, it can delude or liberate, depending on one's insight and intent.

Now if cyberspace is so potentially spiritual, what about the commercialization and exploitation of the net for greed and hatred? What about cyber-terrorism? We should be no more surprised by the "samsara" (illusion) online than about the rampant delusion in the "real" world. All the predictable mind factors are present in all possible regions that human consciousness can pervade, including the modern marketplace and the media of TV, radio, film and print. Digital communications is simply the next manifest extension of the collective mind, reflecting the "worst" and "best" of human capacities and endeavors, our past as well as our potential.

What is most intriguing is the possibility of using this new transpersonal, omni-dimensional, spontaneously morphing intellisphere to swiftly facilitate large-scale improvement in the human condition, just when time has become so critical to our collective survival.

The question of Cyberspace having Buddha nature is not just a quaint *koan* (meditation puzzle) suitable for personal reflection. The prospects for the universal dissemination of truth and enlightenment transcend conventional religious concerns. Faced with overpopulation, dwindling resources, and the specter of unprecedented military and environmental destruction, it just may be the most significant issue of our age. As the 21st Century dawns, it is time for the mundane and the metaphysical to be seen as One. If life on earth is to survive, nothing short of a world-awakening will suffice. How can the traditional *sangha* - the community of compassionate spiritual practitioners - contribute to this much needed global transformation? One way is by going on-line, the cyber-equivalent of expanding your consciousness *and* your effectiveness.

Given a tradition of purposeful concentration, it is fitting that Buddhists choose to seize the opportunity for instant global communication presented by the net to preserve and propagate the precious teachings (*Dharma*), to counter ignorance and unnecessary suffering (*samsara* and *dukha*), spread loving-kindness (*metta*), and contribute to the general liberation (*moksa*) of all sentient beings.

This excerpt from a talk given by The Dalai Lama appeared on the metaphysical Web site called The Weaver

> *"It is my belief, for the world in general, that compassion is more important than "religion." The population of our planet is over five billion. Of these, perhaps one billion actively and sincerely follow a formal religion. The remaining over four billion are not believers in the true sense. If we regard the development of compassion and other good qualities as the business only of religion, these over four billion, the majority, will be excluded. As brothers and sisters, members of our great human family, every one of these people has the potential to be inspired by the need for compassion, and that can be developed and nurtured without following or practicing a particular religion.*
>
> *Today, we are faced with many global problems such as poverty, over-population and the destruction of the environment. These are problems that we have to address together. No single community or nation can expect to solve them on its own. This indicates how inter-dependent our world has become. The global economy too is becoming increasingly integrated so that the results of an election in one country can affect the stock market of another.*
>
> *In ancient times, each village was more or less self-sufficient and independent. There was neither the need nor the expectation of cooperation with others out-side the village. You survived by doing everything yourself. The situation now has completely changed. It has become very old-fashioned to think only in terms of my nation or my country, let alone my village. Universal responsibility is the real key to overcoming our problems. "*

Lonny J. Brown

In his book, *Violence and Compassion* (Doubleday, 1996), His Holiness elaborates on the vital union of religion and science: *"We need a new concept, a lay spirituality. We ought to promote this concept, with the help of scientists. It could lead us to set up what we are all looking for, a secular morality. I believe in it deeply. And I think we need it so the world can have a better future.*

One working metaphor for the Great Matrix of cyberspace is the universal sensorium known in esoteric traditions as the *akashic records*. In this metaphysical realm, - unlike in material, "atom-based" repositories - once information is impressed into memory, it "lives" virtually, forever (sort of like the Mind of God.)

It is now apparent that the omnipresent, instantaneously interactive electronic super-structure of the internet/ World Wide Web, and all the omipresent electro-etheric information systems - the mega-data banks, digital cellular/fiber-optic satellite-relayed telephone networks, plus TV, FM, AM and amateur radio, citizens bands, microwaves and myriad spectral realms, - collectively comprise the evolving sentient nervous system of the planet. Cyberspace is our emerging planetary super-consciousness. *The multi-dimensional link-up we are undergoing amounts to nothing less than the emerging world self-awareness.*

This is cause for optimism and enthusiasm. We may soon be seeing the first moment in history when at least most people most of the time realize their underlying Unity with everyone else and the world, *and begin to behave accordingly.* To quote a June, 1994 issue of *Scientific American,* "Computer networking offers the soundest basis for world peace that has yet been presented. Peace must be created on the bulwark of understanding. International computer networks will knit together the peoples of the world in bonds of mutual respect; its possibilities are vast, indeed."

ENLIGHTENMENT ON-LINE

Can a person become enlightened by going on-line? Well, yes and no. This is not a treasure hunt in the sense that "The Truth that Sets You Free" can be located at some specific Web site and downloaded like another e-market commodity. That's just the electronic equivalent of what the Tibetan teacher Chogyam Trungpa Rimpoche called "spiritual materialism."

As in traditional pilgrimages, the essence of spiritual web surfing is in the journey as much as the destination. In fact, there is no "place" there, which - again paradoxically - is one of the enlightening aspects of the virtual world: it's

126

everywhere and nowhere. It is an altogether different, but omnipresent dimension that we experience only by venturing beyond ourselves.

Let's define some terms.

"Information," in the most complete sense means *traces of intelligence,* from DNA coding to cave drawings to computerized databases. Today's electronic information repositories includes all the keyed-in, scanned, recorded and transmitted messages, all satellite signals, all music and video recording, stored images, the knowledge contained in all on-line libraries... This mushrooming digitized, interactive *meta-memory* is already intrinsically and inextricably linked to human consciousness in ways which we can now only begin to imagine. Hopefully, one of those is the enlightenment of humanity.

Information becomes "knowledge" whenever it enables us to see more clearly and understand ourselves and the Universe. Ultimately, knowledge leads to wisdom, through which living Spirit expresses itself in life.

But just what is "spiritual" anyway? And how would I recognize it in the vast full/emptiness of Cyberspace? Is there not even more room for pseudo-truth and self-deception out there in the etheric foam of the digital sea?

One man's spirituality may be another's blasphemy. That's what is so remarkable about the cybernetic approach to the Eternal Quest: It is at once pluralistic, democratic and personal. You're not limited to any preprogrammed package of goods or anyone else's idea of what you should think, know, believe or discover. All ideas, philosophies, practices, religions, sects, teachers and texts await your consideration.

Of course the price of this on-line eclecticism is the potential for more dilettantism, delusion and confusion. Does the fool who persists in his folly eventually becomes wise? The saving grace of Cyberspace may very well be that it can greatly accelerate the learning process. Perhaps all this religious freedom will lead to just enough enlightenment.

This much we know: true spirituality is not an *appearance,* no matter how brilliant; or a position, no matter how venerable. In Cyberspace as in life, we should know the genuine article unequivocally, by its effects: What *good* is it? Quite simply, something (or someone) is spiritual if his/her/its influence actually reduces human suffering and increases freedom: not only freedom from fear, ignorance, shame, guilt, hunger, and pain, but freedom *for* growth and realization. It's not enough for a teacher (or teaching) to sound good. If it's authentic, by definition it benefits people and the planet. If it's enlightening, the soul stirs and the spirit soars from the contact, as if lifted by angels.

What is "Enlightenment?" In our personal, "relative reality," it is the only alternative to the neurotic prison of the personality, the tight container of all our fear and greed and pain. In society, enlightened consensus and policy will replace violence with compassion in our hearts and homes, and translate into equal opportunity in our schools, neighborhoods, cities and nations. Enlightened action within a global/historic context is our best chance of stopping military warfare and averting environmental catastrophe.

Ultimate Enlightenment may be the full comprehension and experience of the omni-pervasive spaciousness of all phenomena and the full expression of the creative power this insight bestows.

This is not some *thing* that you can get from someone or some place. Yet certain people and places can definitely contribute to the requisite spiritual context, and be conducive to its realization and sustenance, like fertile soil to a dormant seed.

So it is not the content of Cyberspace alone that liberates (although we may deliberately chose "spiritual" sites), but the actual *conscious, purposeful participation in the phenomenon itself.* If you can fully experience and realize the true significance of the "World Wide Web," it does not matter if you're reading the electronic Tao Te Ching, tracking your stock market portfolio or viewing porn sites... it's all *samsara* (illusion) which is just another form of nirvana (enlightenment). It all depends on how you connect. *To log on is to break through the limitations of time and space, and potentially, self and other.*

In a complex interactive, multi-dimensional feedback process between creator and creation, the accumulated knowledge-base of the digital realm is also continuously being downloaded back into human consciousness. How will this affect our precarious collective destiny? The early, formative stages of the blossoming of the Cybersphere are when we have our greatest leverage on the future. What shall we create with this information-age equivalent of atomic power? An explosion of trivia and babble leading to psychic meltdown? Or a Web of Wisdom that enlightens us and not coincidentally saves the world?

For the first time in history we now have the option of deliberately manifesting and participating in a dynamic fabric of mutually-interactive intelligence for the benefit of all. The result of connecting up the network of awareness is *synergetic*: far more than merely the sum of its parts. When a critical mass of complexity and connections are achieved within the system, a flashover *phase transformation* occurs, like carbon under pressure becoming diamond. We participate in and *become* the larger awareness, the evolving self-consciousness of Gaia, the emerging super-intelligence of the Earth Herself. To update the pop aphorism of the psychedelic age, *Turn on, Tune in, and Wake Up!*

The Chinese Book of Cyber-Changes

If you meet the Buddha on the info highway, merge!
Gary Ray, CyberSangha

For all their complexity and power, computers - even the most sophisticated - - accomplish their invisible digital tasks through the micro-electronic alternation of only two basic functions: on or off. One or zero. Yes or no. Positive, negative. This most elementary signal structure enables vast amounts of information to be squeezed through those skinny phone lines and bounced off satellites: It's all streams of pulses and pauses in the great energy omni-circuit.

Five thousand years ago, Chinese sages recognized that nature itself (the Tao) behaves in a similar binary fashion, and wrote an interactive "program" based on this knowledge, called the *I-Ching*, the *Book of Change.*

The Taoists called the opposing forces that "make the world go 'round" Yin and Yang, reflected in natural life as female and male, cold and heat, electron and proton, moon and sun, contraction and expansion, heaven and earth, and every other possible set of dualities in creation. Perceiving the play of natural patterns in which these complimentary opposites interact leads to universal understanding. The *Book of Change* reveals these universal dynamics with timeless grace, and makes them personal and practical.

In something of a historic accomplishment, this ancient psycho- spiritual self-reflection aid - possibly the oldest recorded text in the world - has been quite effectively transposed into the modern idiom of telecomputing. The result is a fascinating blend of old and new, Eastern and Western expertise by which an ancient source of wisdom has become virtually omnipresent and simultaneously instantly accessible to almost anyone anywhere.

Tao on a Chip
There is good reason for the durability of the *I Ching* as a source of guidance spanning the continents and centuries. It is a unique conduit for natural insight that is universally applicable. Anyone who has ever "cast the *Ching*" three times or three thousand times will tell you it always seems to be uncannily pertinent, almost eerily accurate. Which is why it is called an Oracle, a device for "divining," or mirroring the unique synchronistic confluence of all possible variables at any given moment, in any situation. It's "reading" accords with the ways of nature, and is therefore always correct.

It is a testimonial to the book's enduring relevance that it can now be consulted electronically, via the Internet, the great global knowledge repository of the 21st Century. After all, it is called the *Book of Change*, and the emergence of Cyberspace may very well prove to be one of the most monumental changes in the history of our civilization.

Purists will at first be skeptical, contending that using a modern machine to reveal the living teachings of the elders and nature's own truths - instead of the traditional slow tactile ritual of casting coins or meditatively sorting yarrow stalks - would destroy the essential connection that makes the *I Ching* experience so personal. But the critical medium for the message is really the mind of the receiver. The act of logging in can be just as meditative, and - considering the countless unknown forces that affect the ultimate timing of your connection - equally as cosmic.

The online *I Ching's* host computer effectively performs the equivalent of dropping three coins, "heads-or-tails," a million times per second. Whether you use coins, yarrow sticks, or a remote random number generator program, you frame your question carefully, and be as receptive as possible to the answer.

It comes in the form of a Chinese pictograph, one of 64 possible hexagrams, (digital codes) composed of six solid or broken lines, symbolizing your particular predicament at the moment. Your "answer" is further individualized through sub-permutations, called "changing lines," and a second hexagram, reflecting the fundamental Taoist/Buddhist principle that everything is in a constant state of flux. A written interpretive commentary accompanies each reading, discussing the ways of nature and giving specific, if allegorical advice. The guidance is no more or less useful than your openness to it, but even sceptics are often pleasantly startled by the *I Ching's* germaneness to their situation.

SPIRITUAL PEST CONTROL

Non-violent protest is a noble pursuit with a distinguished history, from Mahatma Gandhi's independence movement in India, through the American civil rights accomplishments to recent bloodless revolutions in Eastern Europe.

In garden ecology, proactive non-violence is demonstrated by employing companion planting and natural predators in lieu of toxic chemical pesticides. (From a holistic point of view, it is not surprising that such cooperative agriculture yields the healthiest and most delicious produce.) In the cultural-legal arena, the rights of animals, and even those of trees have become public issues, as we continue to question our aggressive heritage and destructive tendencies.

But where do we draw the line in the spirit of cooperation with the wild kingdoms? For most of us it's at our front door. We may be assimilating some eastern attitudes, but it's highly unlikely that many Americans will develop the kind of total passive acceptance that has made cows in the streets of Calcutta as omnipresent as people. Reverence for life is fine, but co-habitation with bovines, insects and rodents? No thanks.

How then to be spiritually/environmentally correct, when the doctrine of harmlessness (Sanskrit: *Ahimsa*) is at odds with good hygiene?

It was just this kind of conflict that led the residents of the Minneapolis Zen Center to ask their teacher, Katagiri Roshi, for advice. Their zendo (meditation hall) had become over-run with cockroaches, and the odious little critters were disturbing meditators and discouraging visitors to the center. Since, in Buddhism the very first precept is the rule against killing, they were caught in a classic moral dilemma. After silently considering the problem, the Roshi, in true Zen form, refused to tell his questioning students what to do.

Moral Dilemmas

Spiritual literature and lore are full of paradoxes in reference to the taking of life. Most Tibetan Buddhists, for example, have taken the vow of non-killing, and dedicate their spiritual practices to the well-being of all sentient beings, yet they are also meat-eaters. Chen Re Zig, the very ideal and embodiment of perfect compassion, is depicted with a full antelope pelt draped over his shoulder.

In the Essene Gospel of Peace, (a transcription from the Dead Sea Scrolls), after instructing his listeners to refrain from meat-eating, Christ addresses the killing of animals:

> *"I tell you truly, of all the creatures living upon the earth, God created only Man after His image. Wherefore, beasts are for man, and not man for beasts. You do not, therefore, transgress the law if you kill the wild beast to save your brother's life. For I tell you truly, man is more than the beast. But he who kills a beast without cause, though the beast attack him not, through lust for slaughter or for its flesh, or for its hide, or yet for its tusks, evil is the deed which he does, for he is turned into a wild beast himself. Wherefore is his end also as the end of wild beasts."*

For fifteen years I lived in a modest cabin in the woods in New England, with plenty of opportunity to reflect on the man-versus-nature conundrum. My little country home was besieged in turn by black flies, mosquitoes, wasps, mice, spiders, moths by the millions, and an insidious microscopic biting gnat locally dubbed "no-see-ums" that easily cruised right through my tightest screens. For 15 consecutive springtimes this army of invaders offered me their perennial challenge: capitulate or fight.. mayhem or murder. After much consideration and experimentation with a wide variety of tactics, both defensive and offensive, a certain philosophy of pest-control has emerged, which I'll share with you.

What do the Ants Think?
First, we must adopt the enlightened native-American view of the other living creatures as kindred spirits. In truth they are neither enemy nor subordinates in the great scheme of things. All life is sacred and important within Creation's matrix.

Next, acknowledge that the presence of household pests may be telling us something about our households. The ants in my kitchen, for instance, were informing me that my tidiness left something to be desired. They wouldn't be there if my crumbs were not. In fact, I needed to thank them for teaching me to keep a clean house!

Mr. Charles Hapgood, author of *Voices of Spirit*, tells of how, when dealing with a colony of ants in his home, he tried convincing them with reason. For several days he would patiently explain his position to the ants, recalling the liabilities of their continued residence, and the mutual benefits of a speedy departure. Much to his amazement, the friendly persuasion worked, and the insects departed.

Having used it myself, I can vouch for the effectiveness of this approach. Here are a few helpful hints for communicating with ants and other swarming, colonial critters.

As with many species, individual ants are relentlessly stupid, but when functioning as a group they often exhibit a remarkable degree of intelligence. One explanation for this is that the "lower" life-forms have not yet evolved to the soul-stage of individuation, but participate instead as a collective over-entity, often called the "deva" of that colony (hive, nest, den..) It is this trans-corporeal deva which receives the information relayed automatically from its many exploring members, and which in turn responds with group behavioral modifications.

For this reason, one should address the colony as a whole, as if it were one being to whom any single insects are more or less replaceable parts. Then, for example, if a few individuals are inadvertently extinguished during your clean-up operations you can view this as an unfortunate but temporary loss of a minor regenerative appendage of the colony. Tell the deva you are sorry, but you are only doing what you must, and that you hope it will soon cooperate and depart. In this way, the group consciousness will eventually learn the necessary consequences of trespassing on your territory.

Aside from direct confrontation with pests, other means of dissuasion and diversion can be considered, such as pet/predators and compost piles. Animals and insects invariably take the path of least resistance.

But then of course there are the varieties of air-born carnivores such as mosquitoes that are after your blood, not your leftovers. What can you do after you've cleaned, screened, ignored and implored, and still the little suckers refuse to allow you a decent night's rest?

Killing with Kindness

Before getting down to last resorts, this might be the time to mention one of the least used means of natural pest control, "spiritual-etheric immunity." In the East, there are numerous accounts of saintly beings using their higher powers to ward off threatening creatures of every description. The phenomenon has been observed often enough to be accepted as common knowledge in many cultures. Thousands once witnessed one of India's dreaded king cobra snakes glide through a quickly-parting crowd directly to the feet of Mahatma Gandhi, only to pause and bask in his esteemed presence, then retreat back to its forest habitat. And in his classic *Autobiography of a Yogi,* Paramahansa Yogananda recalls being tormented by a swarm of bloodthirsty mosquitoes while only a few feet away sat his Guru, Sri Yukteswar, unmolested, in peaceful meditation.

It is not clear whether such masters accomplish these feats by generating some kind of electromagnetic animal repellent, or through direct telepathy with the creatures, but even making the effort is fruitful.

Intruding pests can reveal much about our habitual conditioning, our attachments and fears, and sometimes about the greater powers of the mind. In any case, a certain sensitivity may be in order during our encounters with non-human "nuisances." The animals, our evolutionary juniors, provide us with the opportunity to practice compassion, a much-needed commodity in this world. The insects are especially appreciable as survival artists of the highest ingenuity. They demonstrate co-evolution with other species, bio-chemical and sonar-communications, geo-navigation, and many other technical achievements worth our study and imitation.

Only after all these possible lessons have been appreciated, and after all other means of pest control have been tried, can killing be justified. This decision should be conscious and considered as often as necessary to keep from developing a callous attitude toward the taking of life. (In colonial times, butchers were routinely excluded from juries, because they were felt to be hardened by killing.)

In such matters it would do us well to take a lesson from Native American wisdom. The Indians and Eskimos, like almost all pre-industrial cultures that live in intimate harmony with nature, teach a proper respect for all life, even - or perhaps especially - during the act of taking it. At that moment (and it matters little whether we're sacrificing a buffalo or a bug), we can kill with compassion or we can kill with a vengeance. Both the choice and the consequences are ours. One experience opens the heart, the other poisons it.

To properly spiritualize a sacrifice, deliberate invocative incantations are sometimes chanted at the moment of death. In Tibetan Buddhism, it is said that any creature that so much as hears the sacred phrase *Om Mani Padme Hum* is assured of a rebirth in a higher realm. By reciting the mantra with this selfless intent, you can turn a mere extermination into a charitable act that hopefully benefits both you and your victim!

Can one then literally "kill with kindness"? The late Isabel Hickey, the grandmother of modern American esoteric astrology, used to provide a convincing example at her New Hampshire summer home. With a twinkle in her eye Mrs. Hickey - who was on a strictly first-name basis with the Creator - would always utter the injunction "Go to God," just before smashing a mosquito!

But there can be no one correct formula for the taking of life. Wise persons of every tradition have agreed that there is a Truth higher than conventional morality, but to be in tune with it, we must be totally awake to the uniqueness of every situation, and the value of each living thing.

Life necessitates death. Every day millions of microbes, insects, plants and animals die so that you may continue to live and breathe on this planet. This constant sacrifice is not trivial. Small and dumb as these beings are, they still give completely the only thing they have, their life. If we are to be worthy of the gift, and continue to grow spiritually, we must knowingly accept the implications of all our actions, and create out of the life and death struggle a meaning that is redeeming in purpose, transcendent in scope and vision. Only then will the knowing of what must be done be in perfect union with the doing.

Lonny J. Brown

ENLIGHTENMENT AND EVIL

*One does not become **enlightened** by imagining figures of light, but by making the darkness conscious.*

- Carl Jung

The enlarging vista of awakening mind eventually meets that which would tend to make one recoil. We mistrust enemies, carry grudges and generally draw the line when it comes to forgiving the really bad people. How could you be ONE with your tyrannical boss, or your oppressive mother-in-law, or worse - the evil degenerates who rob and rape and murder and generally destroy all that is good in life? We feel outraged, insulted, indignant, resentful.

Such moments of intense negativity are great opportunities for awakening, through the transcendence of ego and the transformation of hatred. Emmanuel calls it "the choice for love."

By "love," we do not mean a blind naïve forebearance which perpetuates the transgressions of others. While "taking offense" defines you as victim, and empowers the offender, forgiveness doesn't require passively contributing to the delinquency of the perpetrator. Love is proactive, not a resignation to cruelty and injustice.

Consult your conscience. Face your karma with enemies, rivals, competitors. Examine your heart and find your contribution to the problem and pain. It is not easy to get free of the past, but it's the only way to reach a brighter future. Love does not keep score, although it is not stupid. Even as we fight the good fight, we realize that the greatest battle is within. Even as we struggle, we are free.

136

But What about Hitler?

The gnawing question will hang on through ages of debate and soul-searching: Is there reconciliation on the path of Love with the evil in this world? I've posed it to teachers, philosophers, rabbis, and His Holiness the Dalai Lama (who would have every justification for dispising the communist Chinese invaders conducting systematic genocide in his native Tibet.)

The answer seems to be that "evil" is merely the ultimate extreme manifestation of the deceived self-important ego. "Good & evil" are actually "smart & really stupid."

Such a statement may seem all too facile to us unenlightened pilgrims, struggling here in the apparent-real world of rape, murder, terrorism and war. But the actual enemies are ignorance, fear, and hatred, both within and without. These three "original poisons" of the ego-identity affect us all. There's a bit of the bigot, the greedy, the psychopathic in each of us. The Dalai Lama has said he feels sorry for his brutal Communist Chinese oppressors, as one would for "lost children."

Evil is an affliction that we're all having. It both defies and defines by contra-distinction the egoless enlightened mind. We say, *there, but for the grace of God, go I.* Actually *you have already been there,* many times. Furthermore, you may yet be there again, so capricious can human character be. Judge not, lest you be judged. That superiority you're feeling is a trap that perpetuates what you think you must hate. The best approach to "evil" seems to be enlightened equanimity.

PERILS ON THE PATH

False Enlightenment
The higher you climb, the easier it is to fall. Just when you think you've arrived, you're lost. You get complacent, and become a holy phony. The antidote is uncompromising modesty.

Addiction
The great challenge of our time is addiction. Given unlimited supplies, we can overdo everything: food, drugs, alcohol, TV, sex, money.. You name it, and someone is addicted to it. We have an all-consuming love/hate relationship with the material world, and it's killing us.

A spiritual crisis occurs when habits preclude ethics and good judgment, or jeopardize one's health, responsibilities, goodwill, or freedom. It is not enough to know that moderation is wise. Knowledge needs to be energized by will power. Sometimes the catalyst is a serious loss, or extreme pain. The older and stronger the addiction, the more radical the transformation required.

Light Blindness
Sometimes enlightenment can leave one starry-eyed and naïve. Remember: seeing through your own pain doesn't negate that of others.

ENLIGHTENED POLITICS?

Where do you draw the line between "us" and "them"?

Two bitter enemies with packs of matches face off in a room full of gasoline.. Who has the advantage?

To transcend boundaries, *find that which you hold dear in yourself in the "other," and see that which you despise in the other, in yourself.* Nationalism has become provincial, chauvinistic, and dysfunctional in the nuclear/cyber-age. Peace means Mutually Assured Survival.

JOY IS YOUR BIRTHRIGHT

Effort is there, disciplines are employed, discrimination is used, but the emphasis is changed from an individual seeking power, knowledge and spiritual evolution to a cell in the body of the Universe being gradually revealed its true universal nature. For just as every drop of water in the sea has all the qualities of the sea, every cell in the Universal Being has the qualities of that Being.

Robert Najemy   *Our Universal Self*

Wonder is the feeling that comes from having an empty head and an open heart.

Wes "Scoop" Nisker

The invisible truth is that a million miracles surround us. So unlikely is life and creation itself, in all its manifestations - from the stupendously great to the infinitesimally small - so ingenious and uncanny and awesome is this Universe and our very consciousness which perceives It, that the wonder is we don't walk about in a constant state of awe and reverence. Perhaps our cavalier attitude towards life proves that we are in fact Gods, for surely only a creator can be blasé about his creation.

MORALITY & RIGHT ACTION

Now that my Mind's eye is opened, the vow to save every living being arises in me spontaneously.

Yaeko

Morality is how you treat others. Correct relationship is enlightened intent in action. It means relating to people with honor and respect, and it's oh so hard sometimes.

Right action is not obedient adherence to a set of rules issued by stern authorities, predicated on mistrust of human nature and enforced by guilt and fear. True moral conduct arises spontaneously from the realization of our connection with one another. Selfless, intuitive, without hesitation or evaluation (and therefore flawlessly timed), it is thus a natural door to the greater context known as the Tao, or the Way, in which everything necessary gets done, whilst nobody requires the credit.

The only mastery that counts is self-mastery. The most difficult thing in the world to change is oneself, yet this movement must precede all others. Abandon conditioned reaction in favor of principled pro-action. Excellence is achievable. Success is nascent in the effort.

SURVIVE & THRIVE / HEAL & BE HEALED

Only when the soul, consciously and with the co-operation of the personality, builds the temple of the body and keeps it full of Light, will disease disappear.

The Tibetan, DK

Although numerous methods may be employed, healing occurs primarily in consciousness.

Steven Levine

In the pursuit of higher truth, it helps if your body is relatively fit. Good health and freedom from pain offer the precious opportunity to rise from the survival imperative to the elevated level of great ideas, transformative experience, and ultimate realization.

If you are attempting your quest exhausted, uptight, polluted, constipated, short of breath, and sore all over, the odds are strong against finding any sort of peace of mind. For many, self-repair must precede (or at least coincide with) growth. A pilgrim's well-being benefits from the very life-affirming nature of the quest, and opportunity for spiritual-level development is in turn accelerated by the grace of improving health.

Lonny J. Brown

ALL HEALING IS SELF-HEALING

They're healing warts with hypnosis, high blood pressure with biofeedback, cancer with visualization, colitis with relaxation, arthritis with yoga, headaches with meditation.

New Age

As the mind sciences and biotechnology enter the new millennium, the revolutionary idea in medicine is "auto-regulation:" mind-based voluntary control of metabolic systems for healing and optimal functioning.

Cellular Intelligence: Feel It in Your Bones

Microbiologists know that the cells in our bodies constantly make intelligent, discriminating choices about numerous internal requirements and events, such as temperature regulation, nutrient selection, and immunological defense. It is as if each cell is itself an individual organism - a sentient being, incredibly efficient at its job mainly because it literally *knows* what to do. Immune cells communicate with the nervous and endocrine systems, learn from experience, and even pass on that accumulated knowledge to their descendents. You are accomplishing these astonishing feats all the time, without thinking about it. Remarkable!

Cell Phones

Living cells are psychic. For example, if a minute sample of human heart tissue is isolated from its host, it will continue to beat at the pulse rate of the time at which it was removed. Incredibly, when placed alongside another sample beating at a different rate, the two will soon synchronize. Does this prove that telepathic communication exists at the cellular level?

Such communication also occurs between the individual cells and the organism as a whole. Polygraphy experts Peter Tompkins and Christopher Bird, authors of *The Secret Life of Plants*, have demonstrated that human sperm in a

142

test tube will react vigorously to the donor forty feet away, through three closed doors, when he inhales stimulating amyl-nitrite fumes.

Yogis have long demonstrated voluntary controls over organ function, body temperature, and even tissue repair rates. They do it by "putting their mind to it." The word for direct sensing of interior bodily states is *proprioception*, and anyone can do it.

Good Contacts

Unfortunately, internal body awareness most often comes as the result of distress and dysfunction. What we're not used to doing is tuning in to the pleasant feelings that can arise from healthy, balanced metabolism, good digestion and normal circulation. But because these functions are carried out by the live, sentient cells with which we are in constant bio-electric contact, the process of chemical osmosis and energy transformation that happens in the intestines, lungs, and nerves is potentially available to awareness.

Even though under-use makes internal perception - also known as "somasthetic awareness" - largely a dormant ability, awakening it is easy. Typical methods employed to develop voluntary control over organs and glands include meditation, visualization and guided imagery, hypnosis, psycho-tropic drugs, fasting, oriental self-healing arts, yoga, and most recently, biofeedback.

Total Recall

Of course it is a great convenience to not have to always consciously attend to the complex processes of digestion and the myriad other metabolic functions. Such a preoccupation would leave us little attention for anything else! To "rise above" cellular consciousness, we evolved a frontal brain lobe and left the autonomic nervous system on automatic. This enabled us to develop higher intelligence (as individual humans), socialization (as families, communities, etc.), and eventually, spiritualization. (Notably, the emerging new holistic paradigm sees each of us humans as cells in the planetary body, Gaia.)

What has been forgotten is that we can still - with the necessary re-education of our senses - focus consciousness back "down" into the cellular level. The ability to "get in touch" like this is a great boon for purposes of self-healing and disease prevention. Researchers have demonstrated that once a cancer patient can sufficiently concentrate on his or her own white blood cells, they can successfully improve immune responses. Migraine sufferers who can learn with biofeedback to lower their hand temperature by a few degrees can effectively reverse the headache at the onset stage. Significantly, it is only by warming the hand from within, *with the mind*, that the method reduces the pain; soaking the subjects' hands in hot water has no such effect.

Mind Medicine

In their book, *Beyond Biofeedback*, Elmer and Alyce Green tell of a cancer patient who learned through hypnosis and visualization how to "sense" the location in his brain of the controls that regulate blood flow: "When asked what it looked like, he described something like a boiler room full of pipes, or perhaps the inside of a submarine. There were valves, switches, and control levers." At the doctor's suggestion, he located the specific controls of the blood supply to the tumor in his bladder, and shut it down. Within a week, the tumor had shrunk considerably, and the "terminal" patient was discharged from the hospital.

Beyond Placebo

Psycho-somatic healing involves non-physical capabilities such as belief, expectation, self-image, imagination, will power, faith, and the full range of possible mental, emotional, and spiritual states. Mind-based healing is not a new idea. The field of placebo research has been systematically investigating the role and power of belief in healing for over a century. Placebos, in effect "trick" the patient into healing herself. But we are now exploring the underlying powers which placebo so dramatically taps. Voluntary self-healing is about to become a full-fledged science.

Today, consciousness-based therapies such as autogenic training, biofeedback, meditation and visualization offer risk-free, low-cost alternatives to chemical drugs for migraine headaches, hypertension, chronic pain, and a variety of stress-related disorders. Soon, hospitals will routinely provide meditation classes, sensory deprivation tanks, and healing environments which use special color schemes, live plants, mood-enhancing music and even virtual-reality healing.

All of these methods radically shift the focus of attention in healing from medicines to the mind. The approach, sometimes called Attitudinal Healing, operates within the intangible domain of our thoughts, yet demonstrates profound physical influence on brain and organ function, cell development, hormonal balance, muscle tone, circulation, temperature, and other physiological indicators. Indeed, no thought or emotion occurs without a corresponding change, subtle or gross, in the physical body. The new medicine capitalizes on this correspondence with precise, easily learned, mind-based, self-healing techniques.

Internal Pharmacy

The late Norman Cousins, author of "Anatomy of an Illness," pointed out that the brain is the largest gland in the body - a "natural apothecary." In the last decade we have discovered a host of mood-modifying chemical neuro-transmitters that are secreted selectively into the nervous system and blood supply in response to messages from the body/mind complex. They profoundly influence both our experience and performance in the world. Some of these chemical catalysts are released at times of emergency and stress, others are triggered by peak sports activities, religious experiences, and internal self-regulatory techniques such as yoga and meditation.

These potent organic compounds account for, among other things, the experience of "runner's high," and that thoroughly pleasant glow we feel after a good round of belly laughter, or orgasm. For pain control, they trigger the body's own built-in morphine supply, called opiods. In a complex chemical balancing act within the brain, the hormones directly affect the efficiency of the immune system and other metabolic functions, rendering cancer, arthritis, and some blood diseases - including hemophilia - responsive to mind-based therapies.

In recognizing the mutual interdependence of mind and body, we are realizing that physiology and psychology are not completely separate sciences. They are merging in holistic medicine, which excludes neither the biological nor the psycho-spiritual dimensions of life. We are whole. The task is to actualize our understanding of this wholeness for practical self-healing.

Self-Healing From Within

The treatments of choice for stress-related disorders (hypertension, migraine headaches, gastrointestinal dysfunctions, and 80% of our common complaints), turn out to be the same consciousness-raising practices which evolved out of the oldest contemplative spiritual traditions on earth: yoga, meditation, breathing exercises, healing visualizations, fasting, prayer. Clinics of the future will undoubtedly include such mind/body training in their range of therapeutic options. Eventually, it may be commonplace for your doctor to instruct you to meditatively "increase your oxygen consumption, reduce the inflammation, lower your blood sugar, and call me in the morning."

HOW TO HEAL YOURSELF

The best way to live a long life is to get a serious ailment and take care of it.

Sir Wm. Osler, MD

- ## Care Enough to Take Care of Yourself
Love yourself, as you are. Release unworthiness, guilt, shame, fear. Forgive yourself, as you know God does.

- ## Listen and Learn From Your Body
Pain and dis-ease are valuable messages - your body-wisdom's attempts to contact your conscious mind. Initiate the vital dialogue with your internal ten-billion-year-old genetic designer.

- ## Save Yourself, It's Later Than You Think
Snap out of it. You know what you need to do. Get in shape: Eat Better! Exercise! Relax!

- ## Enlist support
Get Help. Re-Evaluate Your Life Do it for yourself, for Life. You're worth it.

- ## Comply With Natural Law.
If you want to live a long, healthy life, begin immediately and never stop. Follow your heart-dream. Dare to become your best. Make a deal with God, then keep it. Surrender.

- ## Understand your karma.
Discipline and sacrifice become freedom and deliverance.

- ## Practice Health At All Times
Visualize success. Have good goals for good reasons. Take your vitamins. Call your mother.

SACRED SEX

*By the same acts that cause some men to burn in hell
for thousands of years, the Yogin gains his eternal
salvation.*

Tantra

For a thousand years in the West, the authoritarian male-dominant Christian strategy and edict for handling the emotions, the body, pleasure, and our most *basic instincts*, was to keep them well in check, and generally disavow as best we could any feelings below the waistline. Freud said that empires were built on the resulting sublimated sexual energy.

But the game is over. It turns out there's nothing unspiritual about pleasure, and it's really good for your health.

It is instructive to ask just how we ever came to feel so bad about feeling good. The passions are so overwhelmingly powerful that some religions have been warning us away from them since the dark ages. The heightened intensity of the sexual experience instantly convinces us that it is the most important one in the world. We get carried away, and begin to believe that the next great orgasm is the only important thing in life. People use each other for lust. When we can't handle our attachments, they enslave us and we in turn abuse others. The most extreme consequence is rape.

SURRENDER

The paradox of sex is that the same act can both liberate and imprison. It all depends on your intent, state of mind, conditioning. Sex can drive us either towards or away from Enlightenment.

The great alchemy of love is to transform the trap of addictive physical appetite into the ecstatic realization of Divine Union. It all depends on your true and underlying purpose. It calls for constancy and commitment to the ultimate goal of enlightenment.. and, oh yeah, the death of the ego.

Why is the exhalted gift of lovemaking so often little more than a desperate groping for glandular stimulation in dark rooms, accompanied by feelings of hunger and shame? Ironically, and all too often - when people use each other uncaringly - this most universally accessible mystical experience of sexual love and ecstatic orgasm is debased into something dishonorable and dirty.

But anti-sex admonitions in turn only give rise to guilt, when - despite heroic efforts to curb our "lower appetites" - we find ourselves indulging in what is, after all, the single most compelling human urge after breathing and eating. We might even say that unsuccessful suppression of this primal biological imperative *creates* rapists and pedophiles.

Sexual shame is taught by "authorities" who can embrace neither their animal nor their spiritual nature. They fear one and fake the other, and call this "correct."

Some religious purists still contend that sex must be solely for insemination and procreation, or it is sinful. But obviously the Good Lord made this pro-creational pleasure-drive far more powerful than most individual's (and any church's) power to control. A truly relevant and realistic religion would teach us how to consecrate our sexuality, not repress it. The task now is to unlearn our guilt about wanting sex, while realizing - even celebrating - its seductive nature.

Of course men and women compromise their morality and good judgment for sex all the time (although probably no more than for love, money, power, or fame). But the inherent dangers are hardly reason to forego the rewards. Respect for that very danger should make us take care as we take pleasure. Let us celebrate and make sacred our natural, innate sexuality. Copulation as high communion? Is there any better way?

SEXUAL SPIRITUALITY

What is sought in the Yoga of union is a quality of relationship into which each partner enters fully in order that both may be liberated simultaneously. This level of intimacy is not easily achieved. Therefore, often a man and a woman would forge a life-long spiritual partnership. In other cases a male and female Tantric would go into retreat and practice for a year or two to accomplish specific religious goals together. When the breath, fluids, and subtle energies of the yogic partners penetrate and circulate within once another, they produce experiences that otherwise are extremely difficult to generate through solitary meditation. The texts describe a complex spiritual interdependence, with an emphasis upon the dependence of the man upon the woman and his efforts to supplicate, please, and worship her. Their interdependence reaches fruition as they combine their energies to create a mandala palace spun of bliss and emptiness. Thus, the female and male partners in union both literally and figuratively are ensconced within a mandala generated from and infused by their bliss and wisdom, which radiates from the most intimate point of their physical union. They use the energies and fluids circulating through one another's bodies to become enlightened being in the center of that mandala -

From *Passionate Enlightenment: Women in Tantric Buddhism* by Miranda Shaw, Ph.D. (Princeton University Press)

Many in today's generation are beginning to re-learn the sacred approach to lovemaking, as in indigenous tribal customs, mystical rituals, neo-Sufi and tantric couples practices, and "high monogamy."

Cultures much older than ours have evolved ways for seekers to include the physical pleasures within the context of spiritual practice and the enlightened life. Meditation, invocations, breathing exercises, incense, candlelight, ceremonial objects, rituals, music, and potent libations have been used to create a special environment and mind-state in which to sanctify and intensify sexual union. Such careful preparations tend to quiet the neurotic mind and increase sensitivity and sensuality, while at the same time engendering the proper reverence.

The essence of conscious sex is to transform the very energy of your appetite for personal pleasure into one of godly realization, by harnessing your own desire to the happiness, the thrill, and the total fulfillment of your partner. Thus you achieve Unity through duality, by making her (or his) ecstasy your own. Giving and receiving merge, and two become One.

The transformation from ordinary mechanical, confused, guilt-ridden sex to the profound gift of natural/spiritual lovemaking depends upon a broadening of one's focus from the genitals to the heart, from passion to compassion. Spiritualized sex opens you at all centers at once, animal to divine. Through no other human activity save dying is the opportunity for ego-loss, transformation and transpersonal realization so prevalent and powerful as in conjugal love-making.

On the direct path of conscious awareness - *The Path With No Obstacles* - sexual union naturally also means the union of the continuing practice and its realization. This is what the West has come to refer to as Tantric love. Ultimately, *tantra* means that all experience, thought, and action become the energy of spiritual liberation itself.

The high art of making True Love is mystical and miraculous beyond comprehension. It inundates your entire being. It delivers you - body and soul - to unimagined heights of ecstasy. The discovery of the key to the union of spirituality and sexuality is at once a path to, and a gift of Enlightenment.

The ultimate consummation of physical love-making is complete transcendental union. It bestows upon the lovers the experience of a spectacular breakthrough to the Infinite - beyond, but concurrent with their mortal existence. What begins as duality and polarization within time, climaxes as a shared soul-merging experience of Eternity. A transformation occurs which evolves from desire and passion to a level of total and perfect bliss otherwise rarely known in human existence.

Spiritual merging in love is the elusive prize that everyone seeks when they lay down with another, whether they know it or not. Lust is only a call to love, but who knows how to answer it? We may think we are content giving and taking personal gratification, yet all the while the body/mind/heart seeks nothing less than to lose itself absolutely in love, and be consumed in ecstatic union with the Universe through the beloved.

How to achieve such divine deliverance with one of the most common "animalistic" functions we perform is the secret known to enlightened lovers as the direct path of Love. It transcends the trap of the ego-self: In effect, the world's greatest aphrodisiac is selflessness.

*The point of giving her sexual pleasure is to awaken the
bliss that she will then combine with meditation on
emptiness in order to attain enlightenment.*

Miranda Shaw, Ph.D.
Passionate Enlightenment: Women in Tantric Buddhism

Transcendent love is a religious experience. Your partner becomes a Goddess or God, whom you worship in awe. Every touch is The First, and time stands still. The senses are magnified a thousand fold. You notice everything, and it all conveys tremendous meaning and potency. Foreplay is truly playful, and breathtakingly tender. The pleasure is immediately and continuously perfect, the passion intense and profound. Time itself disappears; the Holy Universe is seen without and felt within as breathtakingly miraculous.

Opening all your centers, engaging all your faculties, the animal/emotional/spiritual crescendo of love lasts forever, and the climax is an exquisite explosion of the body, heart and soul in a spectacular shared revelation of the Universal Being. The after-glow of such a transcendent physical union endures for days.. weeks.. more. The experience is healing and unifying in every way.

HOW TO MAKE ENLIGHTENED LOVE.

- ❖ Timing is everything. Wait for the perfect moment.
- ❖ The strongest aphrodisiac is abstinence.
- ❖ Consecrate the setting. Make it holy/beautiful.
- ❖ Purify yourself in body and mind. Meditate.
- ❖ Dedicate the experience to your highest purpose.
- ❖ Invoke the Goddess of Love.
- ❖ Begin motionless and in silence.
- ❖ Gaze into each other's eyes, long and deep.
- ❖ Breathe together.
- ❖ Feel Inner Guidance.
- ❖ Reside always at the beginning.
- ❖ Energy-aware, move in slow motion, with reverence.
- ❖ Worship your lover. Touch only in awe.
- ❖ Trust your body's deepest impulses.
- ❖ Give voice to your feelings.
- ❖ Make love with your whole being.
- ❖ Transpose taking and giving.
- ❖ Decelerate until time stands still.
- ❖ Abandon all gain and control.
- ❖ Fall in love. Stay in love. Die into Universal Love.
- ❖ Be reborn together, as pure Love in the world.

EXQUISITE LOVE

To lose the self in love, look always to the beginning and keep to the beginning.

Worship each other's pure essence as Goddess and God.

Everything matters.

Use all senses.

Read your beloved's mind/body.

In slow motion abandonment of time itself,
Give only pleasure and love, letting hers become yours, ours.

Surrender continuously, unconditionally,
to the sacred fire within, all consuming, all purifying, all fulfilling.

WHY DEATH IS NOT A PROBLEM

What we call "dead" is an abstraction.
Bohm

*Liberation arises at that moment in the after-
death state when consciousness can realize its
experiences to be nothing other than mind itself.*
Kalu Rinpoche

It has been several years since I began this book, and wrote about my dying mother. She passed away in my arms, and it was good. At 72, she had enjoyed all the blessings of a rich, productive life, touched lots of lives and left at peace with this world.

It turns out my dear mom left her own writings for us. We read them as we scattered her ashes into the cool Caloosahachi river in south-west Florida. At her request we floated purple balloons in the pool.

Nowadays, I think about my mom more than ever. Sometimes I feel her spirit nearby. All my life she gave me the feeling of being absolutely accepted in this world - the unconditional love that only a mother can convey.

THE FALLACY OF PERSONAL FINITUDE

*Even though you live for just one day, if you can be
awakened to the truth, that one day is vastly superior to
an eternal life... If this one day in the lifetime of a
hundred years is lost, will you ever get your hands on it
again?*
Eihei Dogen

When I was about ten or twelve years old, I lived and loved my life with youthful abandon. My happiness was continuous and unbounded. But when I began to realize that eventually I would die - that not only all my enjoyment and good fortune, but my *self* would cease - I felt isolated and terrified. I would lay awake at night and contemplate my own demise with fear and loathing. No matter what I did, in the back of my young mind lurked Demon Death, tainting all possible happiness like dirt in food. I hated aging and old age; death made life seem like a rotten trick, and I despised it. It would take half a lifetime to overcome my revulsion about death and come to terms with my mortality. The process of discovering my immortal connection with the universe involved much seeking and suffering, study and meditation, faith and despair. Along the way, I read every esoteric book I could get my hands on, took LSD, studied with Tibetan masters, meditated, and immersed myself in hospice work. Eventually, I was able to solve this greatest of all riddles, and slay the last dragon, Death. Ultimately, it required only that I begin to truly embrace Life, for despising death belies a misunderstanding of the grand design of creation itself.

The vastness of the Universe used to intimidate me, make me feel infinitesimal and lost. These days, the larger It looms, the more thrilled I am to realize my microscopic, yet vital part in It, and I now know death as the greatest adventure and opportunity.

WE'RE ALL TERMINAL

No matter how long you live, your death is always immanent. Is this morbid? Hardly. Life is all the more precious and sweet for being so temporary. But death is not what you think. True, our everyday identity dissolves at death, but consciousness continues right on as sure as the universe does, and - in death as in life - the quality of the experience is all determined by your mind-set. *Understanding how to die teaches us everything about how to live.*

Dying is of course the ultimate solitary task. There may be loved ones at your side to see you off, and perhaps angels on the other shore to welcome you, but in the dark, mysterious passage between, there's only room for one. The journey may last an eternity or it may occur in the wink of an eye; it may be absolutely terrifying or ecstatically liberating. It all depends on the kind of mental conditioning you've lived with.

There is an old Chinese story about a monk who fell asleep and dreamed he was a butterfly. When he awoke, he wondered whether he was indeed a man who had only dreamed about being a butterfly, or a butterfly now dreaming itself to be a man. Death is something like that... waking up from a very convincing dream.

The truth is, this common experience we routinely call "reality" is so engrossing we think it's all there is, and we've forgotten who we really are and where we come from. Death stands for The End, or the Unknown, and we'd just as soon not get into it, thank you. I mean, I may be small and insignificant, but I'm all I've got, right??

Not really. To reveal a secret known to mystics of every age.. death is no problem. In fact, you can die with the very same comfort and assurance that your feel every night when you fall asleep. When you finally wake up from this life, you'll suddenly realize that death was just the end of a dream; a punch line to a great joke told by your own higher Self.

A SLOWER FAST DEATH

> *While living, be a dead man.*
> *Be thoroughly dead -*
> *And behave as you like,*
> *And all's well.*

> Zen Master Bunan

I once read an account of the monetary settlements obtained by the surviving families of those killed in the DC-10 jetliner crash over Chicago some years ago. It seems the relatives of one of the victims were able to successfully claim a significantly larger monetary compensation because their loved one had been assigned a window seat adjacent to the engine that had failed. They contended that, seeing the engine burning and breaking apart, he must have experienced several moments more suffering than most of the other passengers. The court agreed, and awarded tens of thousands of dollars more to this man's next of kin.

The presumption of course, is that knowing that one's death is imminent constitutes a tremendous misfortune. *But who's isn't?* This is a recent, western cultural perspective. It stems from our deeply ingrained fear of dying, and the elaborate denial and avoidance mechanisms we have developed in order to postpone acknowledging our own mortality for as long as humanly possible. This may be attributed to our loss of the sense of connectedness to the universal, our over-identification with the ego/personality and material body, and the blindly youth-centric culture that results.

Today's Americans desperately crave the impossible dream of physical immortality more than any other people. This obsession, coupled with a material affluence that enables us to cosmetically postpone the inevitable and perpetually amuse ourselves with distractions and trivia, makes us carry on as if our tenure on the planet were anything but finite - until the last moment of rude awakening, and subsequent panic. The predicament is all the sadder because it is not at all necessary. The unfortunate passenger in the doomed airliner's window seat may have suffered more than the others, but he might just as well have also realized Enlightenment sooner.

It is a sad commentary on our society that extreme aversion to mortality is thoroughly accepted as the norm. In many cultures, it is considered essential to contemplate one's pending demise, and valuable to have the opportunity to prepare for it. It would do us well as a society if we could develop the same healthy, practical approach to this inevitable cosmic rite of passage called dying.

GETTING OFF THE WHEEL

> *Thine own consciousness, not formed into anything, in reality void, and the intellect, shining and blissful - these two - are inseparable. Their union is the state of perfect* **Enlightenment**.
>
> The Tibetan Book of the Dead

Death represents a singular opportunity to become enlightened because it is precisely when we may look through the veil of our habitual illusions and glimpse how it all is from a universal perspective. Death is the fast track to Truth.

"Conscious dying" is no easy feat, however, due to the myriad attachments and fears we tend to accumulate as separated egos on the physical plane. In dying, the forces of our own confused mind project our most terrifying fears and seductive distractions, preventing a potentially smooth ascent towards the clear white light of self-realization.

In the "worst-case" scenario, physical and mental addictions prevent a discorporating entity from moving on from this world/plane. He or she becomes a "ghost" - an astral entity doomed to linger about old "haunts" in search of familiar gratifications. If the pull is strong enough, all one's creative powers may become directed towards the field of fixation, and one reincarnates there, to play out accumulated psychic momentum ("karma").

Many in the East devote themselves to rehearsing their own departure from this life through renunciation and meditation, particularly towards their later years. It is not uncommon in India for an elderly householder to bid goodbye to family and friends, and retreat to seclusion in preparation for his ultimate journey, the transition to the great beyond.

Lonny J. Brown

Burial grounds are ideal sites for contemplating one's mortality. Meditating in graveyards is a time-honored practice designed to remind us of our own impermanence, and eventually free us from our fear of death.

In Buddhist practice, the transition to death is taken as a rare opportunity to release from compulsive, karmic rebirth, and *choose your destiny consciously*. A Bodhisattva is that exceptional being who achieves the freedom to *not* reincarnate, and yet then chooses to return to this dense realm of confusion and suffering to enlighten the rest of us deluded, wandering pilgrims.

The yoga practice of *pratyahara*, a systematic meditative sensory-withdrawal exercise, can be used as a kind of rehearsal for the death experience. Here the meditator carefully tunes out the five senses one by one, and beholds what remains: non-conditioned awareness itself... unimpeded by material particulars. Western sensory-deprivation technology can also approximate this state of pure consciousness without stimulation, i.e., *awareness of awareness.*

158

TO LIVE AGAIN

The Absolute Subjectivity that can never be objectified or conceptualized is free from the limitations of space and time; it is not subject to life and death; it goes beyond subject and object, and although it lives in an individual, it is not restricted to the individual.

Master Eisai

A good percentage of the world's population, particularly those living in India, Asia, and the Far East, hold venerated Buddhist and Hindu beliefs about the universal doctrine of reincarnation. To understand this concept, it is important to know what is meant by *incarnation* in these traditions, in which the idea of the non-corporal spirit/soul/awareness and the primacy of mind is fundamental. In these cultures, a human being is seen as essentially an evolving soul-entity, taking on, or "generating" a physical form from time to time, for purposes of attending the school of life on the material plane, with all its inherent restrictions and opportunities, lessons and rewards.

In Hinduism this kernel of life (Atma) which passes through long successions of physical forms is seen as an everlasting piece of Brahma, the One Universal Being. Hindus remind themselves not to get too attached to this plane of existence through the doctrine of "Maya:" the divine play of God that creates the illusory nature of worldly appearances.

In Buddhism, the notion of an ultimately permanent, individual entity is refuted. No thing is separate, and nothing lasts forever. But the patterns and propensities that define our experience and influence our behavior still endure for lifetimes. The challenge is to become fully conscious mind-in-matter, an opportunity unique to humans, midway between the animals and the angels in the cosmic evolutionary journey of consciousness.

We have chosen to take on the karma of our roles, and life-in-time, in order to infuse dense matter with conscious ("divine," "enlightened") spirit. The difficulty of this task constitutes the trial-and-error existence we know as life in the world.

Skeptics contend that the doctrine of reincarnation tends to make people lazy and complacent about morality or social conscience. This was probably one of the arguments used in 553 AD, when the Catholic Second Council of Constantinople expunged the concept of earthly rebirth from its orthodoxy. But for those who understand its implications, reincarnation hardly negates the necessity - or the urge - to achieve love and excellence. Indeed, it tells us in no uncertain terms that "what goes around comes around." Although we've all been through it countless times in our long voyage to Godhead/Buddhahood/Enlightenment, each lifetime is naturally the most important, being the culmination of all our past work and growth, and the seed for the direction of our destiny.

UNLIKELY AS LIFE

> *An Eternity of "straying"*
> *still leaves us very much "at home.*
>
> Tarthang Tulku

Perhaps you still suspect that the possibility of an afterlife is highly unlikely. Well, it's no more unlikely than life itself. (Theoretical physicists tell us that the fact that anything at all exists is highly arbitrary.) At the same time we cannot name one thing in the universe that doesn't come and go in cycles.

If you were God, the All-Knowing, Omnipotent and Omnipresent Universal Being, what would you do for kicks? The best possible way you could have any fun that would be at all interesting or novel would be to disperse your awareness into a gazillion separate parts, each making "believe" that it was the center.. not quite seeing how it fit into the whole picture. Then you (..I, ..we, ..he, ..she,..) could watch the drama unfold with great interest (..fear, ..delight, ..chagrin, ..) in all it's infinite variety, conveniently forgetting it's just THE ONE, playing hide-and-seek with Our Self!

All newborn infants instinctively "know" that they are one with creation. They may get cranky and complain, but the newly-incarnated never worry like we "mature" people do. Naturally fearless, fresh from the womb of creation, a baby continues to directly experience its universal nature, at least for a little while, until cosmic awareness gives way to materialism. You don't remember it very well, but you once existed in such a state, not that long ago. The process of forgetting - and eventually remembering - this universal connection, is the story of your life.

LIFE'S LAST MOMENTS

*My separate self ceased to exist and for a
fraction of time I seemed part of a timeless
immensity of power and joy and light.*

"The Common Experience"

Paradoxically, dying is the greatest opportunity to realize Enlightenment in a person's life. The process of dropping the body and passing beyond the present plane of existence presents a unique and highly liberating perspective on the game of human incarnation. Knowing how to die, you can accelerate your evolution, and avoid a lot of unnecessary suffering.

The death of the great Indian leader Mahatma Gandhi - sudden and violent as it was, at the hands of an assassin - serves as an example of true enlightened presence of mind at life's last moments: he bowed to his killer with the name of God on his lips.

Of course, the odds are against achieving such equanimity without prior mind-training. We tend to die as we live. Many souls are ill-prepared for the transition to the non-corporeal state, and die kicking and screaming, as it were, in fear of losing what they are convinced is most important: the personality, the body, and the comfortable familiarity of dense, material existence. Desires, attachments, and fears in life carry into the dying process, making the transition.. hell.

For these reasons, Tibetans offer readings from the *Book of the Dead* to the recently deceased. It is basically a flight manual used to guide the disincarnated negotiating the confusing psychic landscape of the lower astral planes. It's rough if you fear losing everything and don't have much experience standing on emptiness. You see your own worst fears and live your most terrifying nightmares, believing they are real.

In the midst of such insanity and confusion, what is the likelihood that you will remember how to calm down and cut through the bombardment of experience and emotion you are undergoing? Yet it is precisely at this very moment when Enlightenment is closest. *Chaos is the window of opportunity to the prepared mind.* It all comes down to remembering a few essential (dare we say, *sacred*) truths, despite the turmoil you find yourself in: *Stability resides in seeing the essence of all phenomena as empty. Enlightenment is directly and clearly perceiving the void as the constant source of all appearance.*

Unfortunately, there are many obstacles to this liberating view. In death as in life - only more so - mind is the determining factor in defining reality. First and foremost, we manifest our own expectations, be they negative or positive.

Here we must confront our monsters: our own projections of what we have run from all our lives. Here are the illusions and hallucinations we've clung to, populating a hell of our own making.

But here also are our super-natural allies, the personifications of our faith: angels, saints, deities, heroes and relatives who were the objects of our prayers for guidance and deliverance. (On the relative level in which you believe yourself to exist, so do your devils and angels and Gods. Ultimately "You" are All One.)

And yes, we do see at death our entire life in review. Depending on how one conducted oneself in that life, a person may feel aching remorse, or unbounded joy upon recalling the complete, unedited play-back of his or her actions in the world. In this astral in-between time, we review our life's memories, achievements, and transgressions, and judge ourselves in the light of our larger awareness. Usually, it's a healthy mixture of regret and determination. It is from this level that we make arrangements to settle our karmic debts, and proceed to lay plans for our next go 'round on the Wheel of Life.

There are several approaches to exposing the fallacy of personal finitude and making the breakthrough discovery of the peace of mind that transcends all tribulations. One is to realize your mis-identification with your body. Another is to see through the illusion of time. A third is to discover the true nature of Mind, which is the originator of the Universe and ground of all existence. All three ways are worth the effort.

BODY & SOUL

> *As it turns out, few of us have lost our minds, but most of us have long ago lost our bodies.*

Ken Wilber

Although your body permeates your experience of yourself, you are not wholly your body. This statement may seem odd or obvious, depending on whether your orientation at the moment is one of "common sense" or pure consciousness. At times you may feel as though you are little more than packaged meat, waiting to rot. At other times, you may spontaneously perceive your own participation in infinitude, and - if only for a moment - know yourself as the unbounded spirit that grew your body, but is not confined to it.

Sometimes we behave like we are installed in these physical vehicles, like so many taxi drivers putting in long hours, just to survive. We tolerate our bodies as necessary encumbrances, but never fully embrace them, perhaps because we fear their inevitable breakdown. Other times, we identify completely with the body, only to feel betrayed and scared when it wears out. What a bind.

Convenient Boundary
Soon after being born, like most civilized humans, you underwent the necessary processes of individuation. You were introduced to your family, tagged with a name, indoctrinated into your social role, and bequeathed your cultural identity. Forgetting your cosmic origin, you become completely preoccupied with your sensual, sexy new existence.

The accumulating sensory intake of the present vehicle began to feel like the center of all experience. This specified vantage point and particularization of experience over time formed memory, and the reflected focus of attention we call "self."

I point towards my body and identify "me," as opposed to the rest of the world. The conventional and most convenient boundary between this assumed separateness and all others is my skin, which I rightly endeavor to protect and defend, and from which I gain pleasure, pain and a certain security.

The skin, however, is permeable and takes in the "outside" world, as do the lungs and digestive tract. Paradoxically, your particular bodily survival requires that you consume the light, air, water, and other life forms outside "you." Your existence is really an inter-dependent, inter-penetrated convergence with countless trillions of others in the woven tapestry of life, and not at all the concentric arrangement at the center of which the ego perceives itself. Do fish exist without water, or plants without soil? You are what you eat, and you become what eats you.

If you insist on identifying solely with your body, can you say which parts of the body constitute the real you? If - God forbid - your limbs were amputated, and you had an appendectomy and a heart transplant, you would still be certain that you existed. So *where* is this actual *you*?

Many westerners in particular are convinced that their identity resides in the brain, somewhere behind the eyes, while in the East the seat of the soul is taken to be in the belly. But the continuity-of-experience we call "I" simply cannot be physically located at all, because it is a phantom fabrication.

As biologists know, virtually all the cells that constitute your body die and are replaced every few weeks or months by new ones. Yet "you" are certain that you remain "here" all along. So it is when you die.

In reality, your material body is a transient amalgam of chemicals, minerals, and fluids, all fashioned from what was originally interstellar dust, temporarily condensed into a trillion amazing designs by some incredibly imaginative force (which some call God). Seen from the subatomic level, "you" are mostly vast empty space punctuated by bits of spinning light, speeding through the void. So, *where* are you.. and where are *you?*

Discovering that "I am not my body" does not require its renunciation, only the fear of losing it. Conversely, the impossible assumption that the body is an unwanted burden or an evil trap has created schizophrenic, anti-sexual religiosity, and a warped, repressive mentality that kills joy on contact. Better to wear your costume with pride. Just don't try to sleep in it.

The body is the continuous expression of the soul/spirit in matter. It is Super-Consciousness - which is primary to matter - in creation, and "in person." This wondrous, unseen, innate meta-intelligence was able to take up nutrients from your mother's womb and begin transmuting them into cells and blood and bones and living tissue. Some miraculous process arranged the proteins and minerals according to a complex billion-year-old genetic blueprint, and formed your perfect little body: irrefutable evidence of the intelligence of the Universe out of which you emerged.

That cosmic life within you continues to manufacture millions of new cells within the body daily, and heal, rebuild and renew itself for decades. But as it naturally ages, the package of skin and bones which your confined awareness has called home begins to feel more like a cage. Eventually, it becomes the tomb of the ego. Those that have spent a lifetime clinging blindly to an impermanent body and a finite personality, experience death with sheer terror. That is why we are well advised to practice cultivating an awareness of self as psycho-spiritual being - not defined by, but temporarily projecting through - the material form.

If we are not the body, neither can we claim with any more accuracy to be our thoughts. If I am my waking consciousness, who am I when I am sleeping? *If my mind is myself, do I become someone else when I change it?*

Preceding the body is the biochemical genetic design, and before that, the original organizing energy of those patterns. But primary to all elements of your being was - and still is - the unwavering will of the eternal spirit to incarnate, which is the causal "idea" in Universal Mind. Before the Big Bang was the Big Thought. The rest is history, more eloquent testimony to the awesome, infinite creative power of the Tao/God/Buddha-Mind.

HOW TO DIE

*There is really nothing to be afraid of.
Remember the instruction: Whatever you
come across - go beyond.*

How then can a person die consciously, in equanimity, without fear or delusion, into Enlightenment? The answer sounds simple enough, but it requires a lifetime of practice.
The way to enlightened death is the same as enlightened living. The best way to die is also the best way to meditate, to relax, to forgive, to make love, to give birth, to defecate, to urinate, to sleep, to cry, to sneeze, to have orgasm and get divorced: it is expressed in the two deceptively simple words: Let Go.

LET GO of your body, that old friend that served you so well. LET GO of your cherished identity. LET GO of what you thought was important. LET GO of all fears and everything you would grasp for security.. There is no real threat. LET GO of your expectations, opinions, and smart ideas altogether. LET GO of the world as you knew it.
Systematically LET GO of the physical elements: earth, water, fire, air.. Again and again, LET GO of your breath. LET GO of your mind. With faith in the Universe, you can even LET GO of what you think it is to be human. LET GO of every thought and everything you can think of; here even "inside" and "outside" become useless. LET GO until you become letting go, in the ultimate realization that the whole/holy sentient universe is void, omnipresent and perpetual within and without you..

Don't move.
Just die.. over and over.
Don't anticipate.
Nothing can save you now
because you have only this moment.
Not even enlightenment will help you now,
because there are no other moments.
With no future, be true to yourself
And express yourself fully.
Don't move.
Shunryu Suzuki Roshi.

165

TRANSFORMATION

No wonder such liberation in death takes a lifetime of practice. When annihilation, monsters, regrets and seductions inundate you, will you have the presence of mind to ignore the forms and feelings and behold only the Light within? If you are still capable of being frightened, in life or in your sleep, you will surely fear death.

The only way out is through. Stop clutching for safety and you will instantly discover that there is no threat. You need only to *let go and trust,* to see that you are bigger than your whole life, and still within the womb of the Universe. Emptiness is the ground of all being.

In this way, when we absolutely *let go,* it's as if we suddenly realize, *everything is all right, even this very death... You are The Light that shines everywhere.* Dying is miraculously transformed from the most horrendous experience imaginable to the most expansive and beautiful and enlightening. It becomes natural and welcomed.. no more tragic or traumatic than walking into the next room or taking off an old, ill-fitting suit of clothes. Or turning on the light. Ask anyone who's been clinically dead and returned to talk about it.

Those who know advise that we practice now, everyday, in preparation for that once-in-a-lifetime opportunity, to die with mindfulness, peace, and enlightenment.

Ah.. just like that, death becomes the punch line to a good joke, the answer to the riddle of your incarnation. You finally remember that being born and dying are like inhaling and exhaling, and you no longer foolishly wish for one without the other. As if from a confusing dream, you "wake up," in infinity, bemused to discover that there was nothing to fear all along. You expand into complete understanding of the ingenious timeless perfection of All.

So don't worry (even if you can't stop worrying). Death is the surprise ending that makes the mystery make sense. It's the pause that refreshes. And if you're still fond of the predicament you left, you can be sure you'll fall back into it, to continue your vividly convincing, Technicolor, "3-D" sense-surrounding dream of life on earth. It'll even seem like the very first time. How ingenious!

TRUISMS

✧ *You are superior to no one, and inferior to no one.*

✧ *Everything and everybody changes.*

✧ *Equanimity comes with practice.*

✧ *Energy follows thought.*

✧ *Love is all you need.*

✧ *The personal and planetary are identical.*

✧ *There's no time but now.*

✧ *Mind is omnipresent.*

✧ *Emptiness is the ground of all being.*

✧ *Wisdom is beyond knowledge, and closer than your breath.*

✧ *Enlightenment has no form.*

✧ *It's all One.*

MORTALITY AND THE ILLUSION OF TIME.

Time has always been one of our boldest and most ingenious inventions, and, when you think about it, one of the least plausible of our fictions.

Diane Ackerman

People like us, who believe in physics, know that the distinction between past, present, and future is only a stubbornly persistent illusion.

Albert Einstein

Along with the ego, and very much related to it, the other great trick played on the mind of man is the illusion of time. Most of us are perfectly convinced that time exists as a straight road along which we inexorably travel, like so many aging commuters stuck in traffic. Riding from the past into the future, we experience the present in fleeting glimpses... slices of scenery which quickly slip by and recede in the rear-view mirror of history.

Actually - popular opinion notwithstanding - time as we "know" it does not exist. Only the NOW exists. The "past" only exists right now, in our collective memory bank. It's all now. The Eternal NOW is all you ever have of experience or knowledge. We store memory pictures of the changing patterns we perceive all about us, and attribute them to the passage of a phantom quality of reality expediently termed "time." We get trapped in it - unable to grasp the moment, uncertain of the future - we feel like all we really have are our memories, and they are always fading. In this frame of mind, life becomes an endless series of losses, as the body deteriorates and decays right out from under you.

The common convention of gathering one's data about the world through the five senses leads to the conclusion that "everything takes time," and this is "true," relatively speaking. But the cosmic view reveals a different Truth. Eternity is all there is or ever was or will be. So don't worry; just as you realize that the *now* is all you'll ever have, you understand that it's all you ever need. Whatever created the Universe never went away. *It's all still doing it all.*

If you want to know what eternity means, it is no further than this very moment. If you fail to catch it in this present moment, you will not get it, however many times you are reborn in hundreds of thousands of years.

Zen Master Seppo

Here's a mind-stretching time/perception exercise: Suppose you could observe the path of the earth from a vantage point far out in space, over the course of billions of years. From this time-compressed astronomical perspective, the prominent observable feature of the planet would be *not the spherical globe, but its spiral trajectory* ("long body,") stretched out over the eons of space-time. In fact the long body of the earth might appear like a twisted wire, with the silver casing of the moon's long body wrapped around it, like insulation covering a wire. The earth/moon cable would in turn appear (in our ultra-long-term view) as inter-woven with the long bodies of all the other planets, a braided sheath around a brilliantly radiant core which is the sun's own long body.

So paradoxically, the more of the lifetime of the solar system you can behold, the more solid it appears. Ultimately, the spinning disk of the Milky Way galaxy itself appears elongated and dense, like a tree trunk, standing in a dense interstellar "forest" of equally solid galactic light-bodies, all here, all "now."

Because you imagine that time only passes, you do not learn the truth of being-time. In a word, every being in the entire world is a separate time in one continuum.

Eihei Dogen

As with sub-atomic observations, the question of whether some "thing" is matter or anti-matter, "full" or "empty," substantial or ethereal, depends on how much "time" you take to look at it. To a fruit fly, a day is a lifetime and a week is eternity. "Human time" shows only a slightly less myopic cross section of what is.

It may be difficult to break the spell, but with practice, we can see through the false notion of two-dimensional time. The experience is exhilarating, for it constitutes an escape from the forced march of the days and decades. You realize that in essence, you really are immortal, for you exist within Eternity. Truly understanding the non-existence of time is Enlightenment.

What is time.. but the panoramic succession of our states of consciousness?

H.P. Blavatsky

The realization of one's immortality usually only dawns after death - and for the unprepared - only fleetingly and with much tribulation. Such an awakening while still in earthly existence is surely a prize worth winning. With it comes a peace of mind that far surpasses any gratification offered by the temporal/material world. The Zen masters call it the deathless state.

> *To meditate is to transcend time. It is only when the mind transcends time that truth ceases to be an abstraction.*
> Krishnamurti

One classic Buddhist method of freeing one's self from the tyranny of time is to continuously observe and contemplate the universal quality of *impermanence*: The only constant is change. No "thing" is. You cannot step into the same river twice. Realizing that there is nowhere to stand is no cause for dismay, however. On the contrary, when you perceive the universality of impermanence, paradoxically, the whole Universe becomes your native place, happiness your natural state.

> *There is no past, present or future. Using tenses to divide time is like making chalk marks on water.* Janet Frame

Leading physicists also tell us that time isn't what it used to be. Einstein discovered curved, four-dimensional space/time. It is relative to speed and acceleration, and can be slowed down, bent, and theoretically even reversed. Until recently, it was taken as an irrefutable law of nature that instantaneous action at a distance was impossible. Now - strange as it may seem to our 3-dimensional space/time-bound brains - quantum particle physics has been forced to conclude by its own investigations that the properties of one sub-nuclear "event" *here* can determine another, *there,* in virtually no time! Suddenly, our 14-billion-light-year wide universe becomes a lot more accessible. The invisible, impossibly small, fleeting "strings" that may make up everything are more like bits of consciousness then things, which explains the statistical nature of quantum physics: our reality is a consensus of what we're all "voting" for all the time with our attention and intention.

The timeless in you is aware of life's timelessness,
And knows that yesterday is but today's memory,
and tomorrow is today's dream.
And that which sings and contemplates in you is still
dwelling within the bounds of that first moment which
scattered the stars into space.

Kahlil Gibran

REAL COMMENTS FROM REAL FRIENDS

WHAT DOES ENLIGHTENMENT MEAN TO YOU?

Dear Lonny,
Enlightenment? It is how we die and are reborn and die again and are reborn, again and again, and again. In little ways, small ways, subtle ways. Each time shedding another layer, gaining insight, growing a soul. I used to think enlightenment would come quickly, instantly, with the right attitude or correct breath, or mantra.

I hear enlightenment in the city's roar - slow, steady, waiting for me when I am ready to relax the defenses that keep me holding on.

To be continued..

Eric Linter

Here is what enlightenment means to me:
A glimpse of a moment in which one becomes connected with the very source of collective intelligence. At a moment of Enlightenment, the truth can be seen clearly, and many questions find their answers. Enlightenment is also remembering or realizing our true, authentic nature, because the whole reservoir of life experience, from past, present, and future already exists within us. All we need is a quick ray of light to bring it back to our conscious mind.

Orna Benshoshan

I believe Enlightenment is a transitory state. When we experience it, it represents some kind of broadening or deepening of understanding of life, spirituality, knowledge.. It usually is accompanied by our having let go of a preconception about our world or universe.

Mark Peterson

It means having an awareness that allows one to be open to insight.

Pam Bowers

It seems to me that the challenge of Enlightenment in our time is not in understanding our relationship to the divine, but acting on it. Moving from our heads to our hearts and hands - thereby transforming ourselves and the world. That's the challenge!

Virginia K. Slayton

Hi All,
I have a theory on enlightenment. Maybe it is not to defend your beliefs, make judgements on other beliefs, stop looking for happiness, money, love and just work on being good to those you directly experience. I mean what good is putting down religion, all it is really is a way to get to true god within all of us. All we really need is a roof over our head and a baloney sandwich to get through the day. If that can satisfy me I will be truly enlightened.

Al

Enlightenment is the presence of unconditional Love!

Mary

If enlightenment is anything beyond an illusion like anything else in the conceptual framework, I would say that it is the recognition of the presence of an underlying, constant inner peace in the midst of the worst possible chaos, renewed moment by moment, or lost moment by moment, depending on the openness of the heart to the Grace of the One Spirit.

Sandra Koulas Denninger, Rev.
http://yogasandrareiki.byregion.net

TashaHal@aol.com writes:
It is being in the present moment and at the same time in the eternal moment, from moment to moment.

Dear Lonny, You are a good friend! Your enlightenment means a great deal to me - It is our friends that make our days

173

worthwhile - their smiles upon greeting, their thoughts that encourage our own, their inspirations in whatever arts they are devoting themselves to, whether writing books or growing vegetables and flowers in their gardens. Good Luck & Best Wishes for a successful outcome!   Thea Greene

The trouble with enlightenment: No one can tell you what it will be for you. Yet you are supposed to want it. It is devastating for the person you thought you were, yet it is the goal of much spiritual striving. It's a grace, it doesn't come just because you've paid your dues. Like bodies of water, it comes in various depths and has different qualities. Drink a little each day until you get oceanic, until the ocean is in you.

Enlightenment is what your perception experiences when you are free of the fear of loss and free of illusions - Tall order.

Here is a fruitful bundle of thoughts: "I know now that revelation is from the self, but from that age-long memorial self, that shapes the elaborate shell of the mollusk and the child in the womb.., and that genius is a crisis that joins that buried self for certain moments to our trivial daily mind."
(W.B. Yeats)

Christopher (Briggs) Ember

To me, Enlightenment is the questions to live by.
Nancy (Pooky) Hayden

A moment of brilliant clarity, a feeling of intense joy, a realization that we are more than just our physical bodies, we all stand as one, together, and are inter-connected in a manifestation of collective thoughts. it can happen anywhere, with anyone, at anytime......."incredible!"*

kris peters   iamjoy1@msn.com

Perhaps enlightenment is the realization of what makes harmony in our lives and in the world and then starting down the path to make it happen. How fitting to use technology in the process and I have no doubt that the world changes around technology will be even more dynamic than around the rail road.
Deborah Levine PRproseInk@cs.com

Enlightenment consciousness is bringing to conscious awareness all that is in the subconscious and unconscious (of your body mind) and running you without you being aware of it.
                    Christopher Wynter, Fiona Tulk www.anunda.com

What is Enlightenment? That's like asking, What is God; why are we here; how did this all come to be? And today's answer is not the same as yesterday's, and different still from next year's...
Enlightenment is falling in love -- with yourself and with life. Enlightenment is a state of.. being.. in.. love, feeling that love radiates out from you and comes back to you, experiencing that love in every moment, every breath, every action, seeing that love in every person and in all of creation. It's, finally, the end of separation -- union, communion; longing becomes belonging. Bliss, joy, peace. I guess that's it.
Thanks for asking me.
                            Valerie Butler

Enlightenment is being in the "KNOW/FLY" zone. You "know" you're in the present moment and you can "fly" anywhere in an instant! Well, it's a bit humorous but then I think the world could use more humor.
                    Maril Crabtree   www.sacredfeathers.com

Enlightenment is the realization that something is true or untrue. It may occur as the result of meditation or study or conversation with others. Even children can enlighten us or at least trigger an enlightenment. It may also occur "out of the blue," so to speak.
                    Harry Livermore   hlivermo@bellsouth.net

An enlightened person is one who is at peace with him/her self, family, friends and environment. I believe that seeing the connectedness of all life allows us to happily co-exist with

other kingdoms and cultures. When we separate good & evil, male & female, human & other, we are able to close ranks around our sex, culture, religion, species... and consider everything else some disconnected "other." Harmony returns when we once again understand that there is no separation. We are all always connected to the Source.
Celeste Longacre

En-Light-enment simply means remembering who we really are - Beings of the Light having a human experience. This remembering becomes a meditative experience. We remember, we forget. We bring our attention back to remembering, and we know that we are already enlightened.
Priscilla Anne Flynn www.YogaSanctuary.com

Enlightenment: to be filled with light, to comprehend the light, to know the light, to function from the light, to have the light on all knowledge and to radiate the light.
Genevieve Lewis Paulson

Greetings, Blessing and light, Enlightenment is attained when we accept our soul's invitation to return to an infant-like state of mind and being...free of guilt, free of fear and seperation, and back to our natural state of being... love, light and oneness. "
Blanca Greenberg S.C., RMT

Historically, "Enlightenment" has had religious connotations. Enlightenment is something that occurs after much time has been spent cogitating an idea for goals or aspirations. This involves active awareness and the subconscious. Enlightenment occurs when one finally comes upon the answer. For the artist, maybe this process becomes their religion.
Jessie Pollock Dawes

Enlightenment is knowing that everything is perfect just as it is right now. EVERYTHING IS PERFECT JUST AS IT IS! The knowledge of this enables you to live in total serenity and peace of mind.   Valerie Raudonis

Enlightenment, to me, means entering into a loving relationship with a personal God, whom I call both brother and father. For me, Jesus Christ reveals most completely God's love, compassion, mercy and forgiveness. Knowing that God loves me, I can enter confidently into relationships with other to share that love. That love is my Light.

Fr. George Fitzgerald

Hi, Lonny - To me enlightenment is simply "following your bliss" doing in life what you really want to do - having fun in your work and in your play - enjoying nature and the "Universal play" - being guided by the Spirit Within.

Ted Sheola

I like Charlotte Jacko Beck's idea in "Everyday Zen" that it is not about "finding" something but about losing things

Joella Hutchinson

Enlightenment - looking for the best in someone else - not the worst - the mental will power to overcome negative projection and making someone else's life more buoyant - not dragging them further down. Living simply so others may simply live.

Michael Levine

Enlightenment is a process of revealing how you are continually manifesting your experience of reality. By accessing the quiet peaceful still center in the heart of your being you will discover this truth. In the midst of this spiritual cyclone called life, within each chaotic moment there is a deep stillness. This is the center of your innermost being where true spiritual knowledge resides. Abide in this center & you will find yourself manifesting a rich life, full of meaning, clarity, depth and bliss in discovering your connection to an infinite source of love, intelligence & power.

Jafree Ozwald   www.enlightenedbeings.com

Trusting the discovery of one's own creative, intuitive imagination.

Jon Brooks

It has taken me 25 years to learn about enlightenment, and in all that time I've only seen one good description of it. Enlightenment is a force beyond infinity and real understanding that comes upon you when your mind is still and clear. You do not have to be meditating - walking through the woods works just as well. You can feel the force coming towards you. You must remain open to it. It enters every single cell of your body. You will feel a slight vibration in the ear. You will feel totally engulfed in serenity and a form of pureness which is hard to describe.

It will stay with you for a minute or if you are lucky 5 or 10. If it stayed with you for ever, I think you would be in heaven and not of this world. When it is gone you feel totally calm and happy in mind and body and with all of nature around you. You must cultivate your mind through meditation to clear it ready for the visit of this spiritual experience - this can be difficult, and at first a mantra must be used. I can not imagine any other form of enlightenment - there is only one way.
paul.burn@freeuk.net

Dear Lonny, thanks for the question, "What does Enlightenment mean to you?" Still. Life.
Charlotte Bagley Brown

The state of acceptance of what is and ability to, with faith and an inquisitive spirit, see just where it goes..
Dennis SCMassageTherapy@aol.com

It's freedom from fear & suffering, total presence. To be in bliss and amazement at all times. It's knowing without the slightest doubt that God is within us and that our fate and future are not in our control.
Mitch Russo mitchrusso@yahoo.com

In even the most mundane of everyday activities the sense of anticipation, great joy, and discovery of precious treasures of consciousness is experienced, just by being. This is the great Tao, and the truth of Zen Enlightenment.
Cynthia spiritus@mindspring.com

To me, enlightenment means a flaring-up of the light within. The light (God, Higher Power, The Christ, The Truth - whatever) which is never extinguished and which engulfs one in peace with an awareness of oneness with all.

Anonymous

Enlightenment is the eighth stage of Kriya Yoga called Samadhi. It is the final segment of a three-step process in physiological, psychological and spiritual development where the individual sees himself or herself not only as a separate entity but also at the same time as universal. Total consciousness is not magic it is physics.

Kenneth Toy (Swami Jayananda)

Enlightenment is the experience of becoming more conscious to our human condition through the natural process of receptivity to the life-force, Prana. This is known as Yoga, the union of mind, body and Spirit. Our nature as human beings, and our Divine right, is the ability to receive the healing energy known as Prana. Because we are Souls having a human experience, that is... we are energy beings that live in a body vehicle, our minds, bodies and Souls are healed by the inherent consciousness of the universe. In this experience, we become more awake to our human condition. Once awakened, we have the opportunity to feel compassion and forgiveness for ourselves and all of mankind. This is the process of Enlightenment.

Pamela Hollander, M.A., L.M.T. Indigo Yoga Healing Arts. www.indigoyoga.com.

Enlightenment is the ongoing awakening and falling asleep and awakening and falling asleep and... until you recognize the "Aha!" of evolution.

Perry Garfinkel

New and fresh insight and knowledge, usually from an external source.

Paul Sullivan

What I imagine it to be is complete understanding of ourselves and our world.

Lee Sullivan

To me, enlightenment is acceptance and appreciation of everything that does or does not pass one's way in life.

Anon

Enlightenment is a subjective experience entirely, arrived at by developing and following very specific pathways through the bodymind which connect the dots of life experience and reveal the way things really are.

Josef DellaGrotte, Somatic Training Institute
JDelGrotte@aol.com

I'm going to give my therapist $65 and ask her to tell me what Enlightenment is. As soon as I find out, I'll let you know.

Suzette Banner

Enlightenment is so huge and so simple - like all of the mysteries, it is paradox and balance. Moving toward the light through the fear and the darkness, until they become one. Each holding each. Opening the heart to love of many different kinds. Making a journey.

Annie Graves

I teach that enlightenment happens when one is totally aware of ones own Divinity. The veil is then so thin that there is no longer duality. It is then that one can walk in peace and be the light to everyone else. Its like turning on the light in a room; there is no darkness anywhere. When you open the door darkness does not come in, but light goes out. Our light illuminates where ever we go. We can change the world when we wake up to our divinity.

Carol Gader

Enlightenment is a realization in mind and body of the suffering that is at the heart of all existence. Nothing happens before this realization. When we come to this awareness we also come to a crossroads: We despair or we hope. If we despair, we may die short of our potential or continue in the loop of ignorance until we hope. If we hope, we then consent to participate in a life of compassion, a life of trial and error until in some millennium we become perfect hearts.
Peter W. Majoy

Keep your mind open, but not so open that your brains fall out. Steve Heller

Enlightenment, the act of not acting, but being. When one knows, from an intrinsic place, that he or she IS the very same "stuff" of the lowest and the greatest of creatures, then that individual is enlightened and there is no need to be anything other that what one momentarily IS.
Sherry Healy
http://www.visuallyyoursart.com/artists/shealy/sHEALy.html

Enlightenment is being. Cedar Blue Raven

Y'r book is prob'ly already written by now, but I'll tell you anyhow. "Enlightenment: <u>Remembering</u> what you already know."
Beverly Antaeus

Everything is Mind-Made,
Therefore, you come in and change minds.
You move through the halls of power
with Heart.
Dawn June

What Do You Think?

Dear Reader,
   Having read this far, you must have some ideas of your own about Enlightenment. I'd love to hear them. Your contribution may even appear in the sequel to this book.
   Send your answer to the question **What Does Enlightenment Mean to You?** *to* lonny@holistic.com   with "Enlightenment" in the subject.

Thanks for being there!

Lonny

Appendix

The Bodhisattva Healing Prayer

**Through The Merit Derived From All My Good Deeds,
I Wish To Appease The Suffering Of All Creatures;
To Be The Medicine, The Physician, And The Nurse Of The Sick,
As Long As There Is Sickness.**

**Through Rains Of Food And Drink,
I Wish To Extinguish The Fire Of Hunger And Thirst
I Wish To Be An Inexhaustible Treasure To The Poor
A Servant Who Furnishes Them With All They Lack.**

**My Life, And All My Re-Births, All My Possessions,
All The Merit That I Have Acquired Or Will Acquire -
All That - I Abandon Without Any Hope Of Gain For Myself,
In Order That The Salvation Of All Beings Might Be Promoted.**

**May My Touch Or Contact Calm.
May The Illness And Suffering Of Every Sentient Being
Who Sees Me, Hears Me, Thinks Of Me,
praises or makes offerings to me, or even talks of me,
be completely subsided
May they thus quickly achieve true and complete enlightenment.**

The Prayer of St. Francis of Assisi

Lord, make me an instrument of thy will.
Where there is hatred, let me sow love;
Where there is injury, pardon;
Where there is doubt, faith;
Where there is despair, hope;
Where there is darkness, light;
Where there is sadness, joy;

O, Divine Master, may I not so much seek
To be consoled as to console
To be understood as to understand
To be loved as to love.

For it is in giving that we receive,
It is in pardoning that we are pardoned,
It is in dying that we are born to Eternal Life.

Attitude

The longer I live, the more I realize the impact of attitude on life. Attitude, to me, is more important than facts. It is more important than the past, than education, than money, than circumstances, than failures, than successes, than what other people think, say or do. It is more important than appearance, giftedness or skill. It will make or break a company.. a church.. a home.

The remarkable thing is we have a choice every day regarding the attitude we will embrace for that day. We cannot change our past.. we cannot change the fact that people will act in a certain way. We cannot change the inevitable. The only thing we can do is play on the string we have, and that is our attitude.

I am convinced that life is 10% what happens to me and 90% how I react to it, An so it is with you.. We are in charge of our attitudes.

author unknown

185

Success

*To laugh often and live much; to win the
respect of intelligent persons and the
affection of children; to earn the
approbation of honest critics and endure the
betrayal of false friends; to appreciate
beauty; to find the best in others; to give of
one's self; to leave the world a bit better,
whether by a healthy child, a garden patch
or a redeemed social condition; to have
played and laughed with enthusiasm and
sung with exaltation; to know even one life
has breathed easier because you have lived
– this is to have succeeded.*

author unknown

The Optimist Creed

Promise yourself:

To be so strong that nothing can disturb your peace of mind.
To talk health, happiness and prosperity to every person you meet.
To make all your friends feel that there is something in them.
To look at the sunny side of everything and make your optimism come true.
To think only of the best, to work only for the best and to expect only the best.
To be just as enthusiastic about the success of others as you are about your own.
To forget the mistakes of the past and press on to the greater achievements of the future.
To wear a cheerful countenance at all times.
And give every living creature you meet a smile.
To give so much time to the improvement of yourself,
that you have no time to criticize others.
To be too large for worry, too noble for anger, too strong for fear,
and too happy to permit the presence of trouble.

The Invitation

It doesn't interest me what you do for a living.
I want to know what you ache for, and if you dare to dream of meeting your heart's
  longing.
It doesn't interest me how old you are.
I want to know if you will risk looking like a fool for life, for dreams, for the
  adventure of being alive.
It doesn't interest me what planets are squaring your moon.
I want to know if you have touched the center of your own sorrow, if you have
  been opened by life's betrayals or have become shriveled and closed from fear of
  further pain!
I want to know if you can sit with pain, mine or your own, without moving to hide
  it or fade it or fix it. I want to know if you can be with joy, mine or your own. If
  you can dance with wildness and let ecstasy fill you to the tips of your fingers and
  toes without cautioning us to be careful, be realistic, or to remember the
  limitations of being human.
It doesn't interest me if the story you are telling me is true.
I want to know if you can disappoint another to be true to yourself: if you can bear
  the accusation of betrayal and not betray your own soul.
I want to know if you can be faithful and therefore be trustworthy.
I want to know if you can see beauty even if it's not pretty every day, and if you
  can source your own life from God's presence.
I want to know if you can live with failure, yours and mine, and still stand on the
  edge of a lake and shout to the silver moon, "Yes!"
It doesn't' interest me where you live or how much money you have.
I want to know if you can get up after the night of grief and despair, weary and
  bruised to the bone, and do what needs to be done for the children.
It doesn't interest me to know who you are, how you came to be here.
I want to know if you will stand in the center of the fire with me and not shrink
  back.
It doesn't interest me where or what or with whom you have studied.
I want to know what sustains you from the inside, when all else falls away.
I want to know if you can be alone with yourself; and if you truly like the company
  you keep in the empty moments.

Inspired by Oriah Mountain Dreamer, Native American Elder, May 1994

GREAT REALIZATIONS
& ORDINARY MIRACLES

"It is toward this goal of universal **enlightenment** that humanity needs to move. Those who have achieved enlightenment have generally been few and far between. But, if the world is to be transformed and a high-synergy society is to become a reality, such a shift in consciousness will need to be widespread."

Peter Russell *The Global Brain*
Awakens

The world is now too dangerous for anything less than Utopia
    Buckminster Fuller

*I think we are now facing an entirely new era of **enlightenment**, an era of passionate enlightenment, in which enlightenment will not be seen in the old way as detachment, as an escape, as a way of fading out from existence, as a way of being separate in poised peace, but will combine the ancient and original knowledge of the ground of Being with a very radical commitment to life at every point - emotional, physical, political- to save the planet and transform the quality of life on it.*

Andrew Harvey (*Yoga Journal,* 1995)

*A real spiritual friend would never claim complete enlightenment. A great guide might want to witness supreme spiritual and mystical experiences that they had had, but if those were true experiences, they would nave created in that person a fundamental awe and humility before the divine which would make him or her scrupulously aware of precisely those things in himself or herself that had not yet been transformed. Everyone who enters the enlightened field realizes that **enlightenment** is endless transformation. It is not static. Gregory of Nyssa calls this "epectasis," endless opening. Rumi speaks of transformation being a glory that goes on from light to light.*

189

*So anyone who is in the **enlightenment** field is, by definition, aware of all the mountain peaks of gnosis that they haven't climbed, all the love that they haven't grown when faced with this massive, vast, insanely powerful and beautiful presence. What a real spiritual friend is trying to do is to send you wild with love of That. Real spiritual friends are trying, as Rumi is in his poetry, to communicate to you a fatal attraction, not for them, but for That. A real friend knows that when you are nakedly in contact with the Divine Mother in every moment, in every rose, in every face, in every breath of wind, it is much more vast, ecstatic, and transforming if there is no name or form between you.*

Andrew Harvey (*Yoga Journal,* 1995)

All appearance is sheer art, beautiful beyond all possibility of possession. It cannot be possessed but it is entirely accessible. The treasure which our being preserves for us is like an ever-present nectar; it is like an inexhaustible kingdom which is always open to us.

Tarthang Tulku

I was conscious of the reality of power which transcended that of the physical world. Overwhelmed, astonished, and not a little awed by it, and at the same time deeply thankful and comforted, I realized I should never feel 'alone' again..

The impact of this terrific vision was so deep and sacred that I could not bring myself to disclose it to anyone. I felt transmuted into a state of heavenly glory - a kind of intoxication; my body felt lighter and I was more conscious of all things, both animate and inanimate, on the earth and throughout all creation everywhere. If I lived a thousand years I could ask no greater joy and blessing than to have this ineffable experience again.

"The Common Experience"

Enlightenment in Our Time

BUDDHIST MATHEMATICS*

Pain x Resistance = Suffering

Pain x Equanimity = Spiritual Purification

Fulfillment = Pleasure ÷ Grasping

Spiritual Purification = Pleasure x Equanimity

* with thanks to Shinzen Young

BIBLIOGRAPHY

Benner, Joseph *The Impersonal Life* see Robert Najemy, *Our Universal Self* Century for Harmonious Living, *Griva 23, Halandri, 152-33, Athens, Greece.* and newsletter, *Sharing, Fall, '92*

Benson, Herbert, M.D *The Relaxation Response.* Avon Books NY 1975 ISBN:0-380-00676-6

Besant, Annie *A Study in Consciousness*

Blofeld, John *Gateway To Wisdom - Taoist & Buddhist Contemplative & Healing Yogas* Adapted for Western Students of the Way

Bourne, E.J. *The Anxiety & Phobia Workbook* Oakland, CA: New Harbinger 1995

Brown, Lonny, Ph.D. *Self-Actuated Healing – The Alternative to Doctors and Drugs is Within You.* Naturegraphy Publishers, Happy Camp, CA 1988.

Brown, Lonny J. Ph.D. *Meditation – Beginners Questions and Answers* Enlightenment Projects 121-F Old Town Farm Rd. Peterborough, NH 03458   www.holistic.com/lonny

Chitrabhanu. Gurudeve Shree *The Psychology of Enlightenment - Meditations on the Seven Energy Centers* (Asian Humanities Press, Berkeley, CA)

Cohen & Phipps *The Common Experience - Signposts on the Path to Enlightenment.*

Collin, Rodney *The Theory of Conscious Harmony*

de Mello, Anthony, S.J. *The Heart of The Enlightened*

Eliade, Mircea *Shamanism - Archaic Techniques of Ecstasy*

Emmanual & Friends *Emanuel's Book* & *Emanuel's Book II - The Choice For Love*

Ferrucci, Piero *Inevitable Grace*

Field, Reshad *Steps To Freedom*

Gibran, Kahlil *The Prophet*

Goldsmith, Joel S. *The Art of Meditation* HarperCollins Publishers, 1990.

Goldstein, Joseph & Jack Kornfield *Seeking The Heart of Wisdom - The Path of Insight Meditation*
Goldstein, Joseph *The Experience Of Insight*
Goleman, Daniel *The Varieties of the Meditative Experience*
Goleman, Daniel, Ph.D. *The Varieties of the Meditation Experience* by, E.P. Dutton, NY 1977 Forward by Ram Dass
Happold, F.C. *Mysticism - A Study & an Anthology*
Hawking, Stephen *A Brief History of Time*
Helminski, Kabir Edmund *Living Presence - A Sufi Way to Mindfulness & the Essential Self*
Henderson, Julie, *The Lover Within - Opening to Energy in Sexual Practice* (Station Hill Press Barrytown, NY 12507) ISBN 0-88268-049-8
Hillig, Chuck *Enlightenment for Beginners – Discovering the Dance of the Divine.* Black Dot Publications Ojai, CA
Hixon, Lex *Coming Home - The Experience of Enlightenment in Sacred Traditions*
Isherwood, Christopher and Prabhavananda *How To Know God - The Yoga Aphorisms of Patanjali*
James, Wm. *Varieties of Religious Experience*
Jam-mGon Kong-sPrul *A Direct Path To Enlightenment*
Kabat-Zinn, Jon, Ph.D. *Wherever You Go, There You Are : Mindfulness - Meditation in Everyday Life* Hyperion, 1995
Kaushik, Dr. R.P. *Light of Exploration - Talks on Meditation*
Keyes Ken *Handbook to Higher Consciousness*
Khalsa Dharma Singh, Cameron Stauth, Dharma Singh, MD Khalsa, Joan Borysenko *Meditation As Medicine : Activate the Power of Your Natural Healing Force* Hardcover - 352 pages (February 2001) Pocket Books; ISBN: 074340064X ; Other Editions: Audio Cassette (Abridged), Audio CD (Abridged)
Khan, Pir Vilayat *Toward The One*
Krishnamurti, J. *Think on These Things*
Lao Tsu *Tao Te Ching*
Matthiessen, Peter *Living Meditation, Living Insight – The Path of Mindfulness in Daily Life, , Nine-Headed Dragon River* (Zen Journals 1969-1982) (Shambhala. Boston, 1986) *Meditation in Everyday Life.* Hyperion, 1995
Moyers, Bill *Healing and the Mind* (companion to the PBS series) Doubleday, NY ISBN:0-385-46870-9
Najemy, Robert, *Our Universal Self* Century for Harmonious Living,

Griva 23, Halandri, 152-33, Athens, Greece

Naranjo, Claudio & Robert E. Ornstein *On The Psychology of Meditation* The Viking Press / Esalen NY

Newberg, Andrew, M.D., Eugene D'Aquili, M.D., Ph.D., & Vince *Rause Why God Won't Go Away- Brain Science & The Biology of Belief* Ballantine Books, NY 2001 ISBN 0-345-44033-1

Nisker, Wes *Crazy Wisdom*

Ram Dass *Miracle of Love - Stories About Neem Karoli Baba*

Santorelli Saki *Heal Thy Self: Lessons on Mindfulness in Medicine* Bell Tower, Random House, 1999

Shaw, Miranda, Ph.D *Passionate Enlightenment: Women in Tantric Buddhism* (Princeton University Press 1994

Silbey, Uma *Enlightenment On The Run - Everyday Life As a Spiritual Path* (Airo Press, San Rafael, CA)

Smith, Jean ed *Breath Sweeps Mind: A First Guide to Meditation Practice.* Riverhead Books, 1998.

Sogyal Rinpoche *The Tibetan Book of Living & Dying*)

Sole-Leris, Amadeo *Tranquility & Insight - An Introduction to the Oldest Form of Buddhist Meditation*

Swami Satchidananda *Beyond Words*

Tarthang Tulku *Time, Space and Knowledge - A New Vision of Reality* (Dharma Pub.)

The Dharmapada (Sayings of The Buddha) Translated from the Pali by P. Lal.

The World of Zen - An East-West Anthology Ross, Nancy Wilson

Thich Nhat Hanh *The Miracle of Mindfulness: An Introduction to the Practice of Meditation* Paperback, 140 pp. Beacon Pr; ISBN: 0807012327 also available on audiocassette from www.amazon.com

Tsong-Kha-Pa *The Great Treatise on the Stages of the Path to Enlightenment* The Lamrim Chenmo Translation Committee (Snow Lion)

Underhill, Evelyn *Mysticism*

Van de Wetering, Janwillem *The Empty Mirror: Experiences in A Japanese Zen Monastery* NY: Pocket Books, 1973

Watts, Alan *This Is It*; *Meditation - How To Do It*

White Eagle *The Quiet Mind*

White, John, Ed. What Is Enlightenment - Exploring The Goal of The Spiritual Path (The Aquarian Press, Wellingborough, Northhamptonshire, England)

Wilber, Ken *No Boundary*

Yogananda, Paramahansa *Science of Religion*
Zopa, Lama, Rinpoche   *Transforming Problems Into Happiness*
 (Wisdom Publications - Boston)

About the Author

Lonny J. Brown is the author of *Self-Actuated Healing - The Alternative to Doctors & Drugs is Within You*, (Naturgraph, ISBN 0-87961-185-5), *Meditation – Beginners Questions & Answers* (www.SelfHelpGuides.com), and *ecstatic understatements* (www.LonnyBrown.com)

A practicing Holistic Health Counselor, Lonny teaches Complementary and Alternative Medicine, Mind/Body Healing, Stress Management, Yoga and Meditation at hospitals, schools, and businesses throughout the US., and offers holistic health counseling by email, phone, and in person in the Monadnock region of New Hampshire, USA.

His web site also features essays, tapes, books, and links to a variety of integrative health sources as well as Enlightenment web sites.

www.LonnyBrown.com   lonny@holistic.com

Also by Lonny J. Brown:

- Self-Actuated Healing – The Alternative to Doctors & Drugs is Within You Naturegraph Publishers 1988 ISBN 0-87961-185-5 $7.95 http://members.aol.com/Naturgraph/selfact.htm or amazon.com

- Meditation – Beginners Questions & Answers www.SelfHelpGuides.com

- Ecstatic Understatements (Micro Poems) Enlightenment Projects 121-F Old Town Farm Rd.., Peterborough, NH 03458 603-924-0425 www.LonnyBrown.com $21

- Healing - Personal to Planetary (holistic health column collection) Enlightenment Projects 121-F Old Town Farm Rd.., Peterborough, NH 03458 603-924-0425 www.LonnyBrown.com $15

- Journey Through The Chakras (guided visualization CD) Enlightenment Projects 121-F Old Town Farm Rd.., Peterborough, NH 03458 603-924-0425 $19